DID YOU HEAR ABOUT THE GIRL WHO . . . ?

DID YOU HEAR ABOUT THE GIRL WHO . . . ?

CONTEMPORARY LEGENDS, FOLKLORE, AND HUMAN SEXUALITY

Mariamne H. Whatley

Elissa R. Henken

NEW YORK UNIVERSITY PRESS

New York and London

NEW YORK UNIVERSITY PRESS
New York and London

© 2000 by New York University

Library of Congress Cataloging-in-Publication Data
Whatley, Mariamne H.
Did you hear about the girl who . . . ? : contemporary legends, folklore,
and human sexuality / Mariamne H. Whatley and Elissa R. Henken.
p.   cm.
Includes bibliographical references and index.
ISBN 0-8147-9322-3 (cloth : alk. paper) —
ISBN 0-8147-9323-1 (pbk. : alk. paper)
1. Sex—Folklore. 2. Urban folklore—United States.
I. Henken, Elissa R.   II. Title.
GR462 .W53 2000
398.2'097307—dc21   00-011704

New York University Press books are printed on acid-free paper,
and their binding materials are chosen for strength and durability.

Manufactured in the United States of America

10 9 8 7 6 5 4 3 2 1

To
Jonathan T. Henken
pipe major,
cabinetmaker,
antique motorcycle restorer,
and most excellent big brother.

CONTENTS

PREFACE

When we have discussed this project with friends and colleagues, there has seemed to be almost as much interest in how two sisters survive co-authorship as in the project itself. Intrafamilial writing raises more questions than does multidisciplinary scholarship. This book, a discussion/collaboration between disciplines, began as a conversation between two sisters—one a biologist and health educator, the other a folklorist. During weekly phone conversations, we often discussed our work, sharing anecdotes and information each thought would be of interest to the other. When students would ask the folklorist about the biological/ medical possibility of a belief or legend, she would turn to the biologist for help. When the biologist got more attuned to recognizing legends, she would check them out with the folklorist. And so, while we had always known our own fields to be interdisciplinary, we began to realize more precisely and practically how in their overlapping they could contribute to each other. We first presented our work in an article and received enough encouraging feedback to work on a book. Tim Bartlett, then an editor at NYU Press, was very enthusiastic at the earliest stage.

We have written this book for anyone who cares about sexuality education in its broadest meanings—for health and sexuality educators in the schools and public health settings, for health care providers, for parents, for concerned people—but we have written it with a sense of professional responsibility to both folklore and health education. Our aim is certainly not to turn health educators into folklorists but to make them aware of how pervasive and influential folklore is in people's lives and how being alert to folklore may help them communicate better with their students/clients. Folklore, neither quaint nor cute and certainly not the trivial fluff so often assumed, but rather a basic expression of a group's worldview, of the members' assumptions, concerns, and fears, can help educators focus more clearly on learners' needs and understandings. Folklore opens up possibilities for discussion of topics that may be considered too controversial for the classroom but are circulating every day among the students.

As for the question of how two sisters write together, we undoubtedly fall into dynamics—including friendship, trust, and respect for each other's expertise—that have been developed over the more than forty years we've known each other. We grew up in a household that valued scholarship, intellectual curiosity, and good writing; one child or another was often sent on an errand from the dinner table to check the dictionary or encyclopedia to settle a debate. We also grew up in a family that valued puns and other forms of humor; we have tried to restrain the punning impulse, though, we hope, not the humor one. In the end, we drew on this shared approach, managed to blend our writing styles, and avoided sisterly squabbles.

We hope this book gives folklorists another way to show the applicability of that field, that it shows sexuality/health educators another discipline to draw on, and that it invites all readers to share in the pleasures of interdisciplinary scholarship.

ACKNOWLEDGMENTS

We give special thanks to those people who read and commented on various drafts of the manuscript, giving us essential feedback and encouragement: Julie D'Acci, Charles C. Doyle, Adriane Fugh-Berman, Joseph P. Goodwin, Carl Lindahl, and Jan Savage. Nancy Worcester deserves extra thanks for her emotional and intellectual support throughout this project and for her insightful reading of multiple drafts.

Many people generously contributed legends, beliefs, jokes, and other folklore, which we recognize do not necessarily reflect their own attitudes or beliefs. It would be impossible to name them all but we would particularly like to thank the following people for their contributions: students at the University of Georgia, Sarah Agar, Alan Hendrick, Roger L. Janelli, Alison Moran, Edgar Slotkin, Fran Teague, and Johannah Whatley.

We also wish to thank friends and colleagues in the United States, Great Britain, and Australia, who contributed informally to this project. We are both grateful for the support, both direct and indirect, from our departments: University of Georgia, Department of English; University of Wisconsin-Madison, Department of Curriculum and Instruction, Women's Studies Program, and the School of Education Dean's Office.

Some of our early work that led to this book was published in an article entitled "Folklore, Legends, and Sexuality Education" in *Journal of Sex Education and Therapy* (1995, volume 21 [1], pp. 46–61). We wish to thank the journal editors for being open to publishing interdisciplinary work and for allowing us to retain the rights to use our material in our own work.

I

YES, WE ARE FOLK AND WE DO HAVE FOLKLORE

❑

I believe the woman was from Murphy (North Carolina). A few years ago, she started going to the tanning bed because she wanted to be tan by the time she got married. I think she was getting married around April. Anyway, she didn't have time to get a real tan. A few days before the wedding, she started going to the tanning bed three or four times a day—hoping to get real dark before her wedding day. You know, you're only supposed to go once a day and that's not even good for you. Nancy {a friend of the narrator's family} said that someone told her that they found the girl in one of the beds the day before her wedding and she was dead. She had fried her insides. Just think—the day before her wedding.

This story, told by a woman to her college-student daughter, is folklore, whether or not the mother or the daughter knew it at the time. Specifically, it is a form of folklore called a contemporary legend and is not merely entertainment but also conveys a set of messages. In this book, we present a range of folklore relating to issues of sexuality currently circulating in the United States, particularly among adolescents and young adults. We place that folklore in the context of what it reflects about the society that produces it. As authors who come from different backgrounds—one a biologist whose areas of research are health and sexuality education and women's health, and the other a folklorist—we hope to encourage readers to see the connections between folklore and sexuality education, and especially to encourage health and sexuality educators to use the folklore of their students/clients to enhance their teaching approaches. Because of the rapid changes and regional variations in folklore, it would be impossible to present exhaustively all the folklore circulating about specific topics, such as HIV/AIDS or sexual violence. We have instead selected examples that illustrate what folklore is and how it can be used to enhance sexuality education.

Contemporary Legends

Returning to the legend above helps define one form of folklore. Contemporary legends or "urban legends" are narratives about bizarre, unnatural, or ironic events purported to have happened in the recent past, often in the local community, to an unspecified person (the woman from Murphy or there was this girl who . . .), to people at a couple of removes from the narrator (a friend of a friend), or to famous people. Located as they are in contemporary society, they reflect with particular clarity the current fears and anxieties of a group and serve as warnings about potentially dangerous situations, behaviors, and assumptions. The tanning bed legend serves as an overblown (overdone might be more apt) warning about an unhealthful practice. It is also a commentary on the dangers of artificial beauty standards and the risks women take in attempting to achieve them, though not apparently a criticism of the "beauty" industry that promotes such unhealthy behaviors.

Contemporary legends are generally presented as true, though the narrator and audience may or may not believe them. Debates about whether or not to believe a particular legend are important activities, helping the individual and the group determine the range of acceptable possibilities. Moreover, an individual's degree of belief in a particular legend may vary depending on the context, on who is telling the legend, on the supporting evidence (something that happened to the narrator's friend's aunt can be very convincing), and on the reactions of the rest of the group. Legends may be based on true events, but we will not attempt to prove the "truth" or "falseness" of these legends in the sense of whether or not they actually happened. There are authors, such as Jan Brunvand, who particularly focus on tracking down these legends and checking whether they happened. There are also websites that play this role. For example, on one (http://www.snopes.com/), a red dot indicates that a legend has been shown to be false, while a green dot indicates a real occurrence. Although we will not try to prove whether or not these legends are based on real events, we will explore whether they *could* happen. Legends are presented in a conversational style so that they may be told not only by a single narrator but also by a group of people each adding remembered details and evidence (or even the "scientific" explanation of why it can or cannot be true). Legends, transmitted by doubters as well as believers, are passed on in casual conversation, mixed in with news, rumors, personal experience narratives, or sent by e-mail.

The story told above has appeared in many different forms, having "happened" to young women all over the country. The naming of a specific location (Murphy, N.C.) and the attribution to a friend of the amily combine to lend veracity to the story. Some legends are "authenticated" by false reports of media coverage ("I saw it in the paper"; "It was on *Oprah*") and now, with the use of the Internet, many legends are presented in the format of (fake) newspaper accounts, lending the reports greater apparent legitimacy. A story's presence on the Internet can add a certain aura of veracity, as one author (Anderson, 1997) explains:

> With a computer and a phone line, anyone can become his own publisher/commentator/reporter/anchor, dispatching to everyone everywhere credible-looking opinions, facts, and "facts"

> via the Internet. . . . Thanks to the Web, amateurism and spuri-
> ousness no longer need look amateurish or spurious. (P. 41)

"I saw it on the World Wide Web" becomes a new kind of proof of a legend's truth, serving the same function as, "My friend knows this doctor
who said. . . ." As mentioned previously, there is information available
about whether or not these legends are based on real events, but the evidence countering the veracity of a legend rarely carries the weight that
the legend does. A story like the one about the tanning salon has never
been documented but it still circulates freely and is often believed. It
has a long life because it is frightening, refers to a very common practice, seems as if it could happen to anyone (particularly to any of the
young women who are generally the purveyors or targets of the story),
and has a "moral" that resonates with many—women are punished for
excessive vanity.

The impact a legend has on those telling or hearing it may have little to do with whether the story is believed. People may learn that stories about mall parking lots—with a killer hiding in the back seat of the
car or an Achilles-tendon slasher lying in wait under the car or a serial
killer disguised as a kind businessman who asks only for a lift across the
parking lot after generously changing a tire—are really "just legends."
However, that does not diminish the strength of the warning message,
as women carefully look under their car from a distance before approaching and check the back seat before getting in.

What Is Folklore?

Legends are one form of contemporary folklore that will be examined
in this book. Before discussing the ways in which folklore and sexual-
ity/health education overlap and affect each other, it is important to
clarify what folklore is and, perhaps, correct some misconceptions.
People often think of folklore as quaint sayings and customs belong-

ing to peasants, mountain or rural people, or an easily recognized ethnic group—always "others" viewed at a distance, rather than one's own (even if marginalized) group. In fact, folklore is part of every individual's everyday life, no matter how "civilized," westernized, urbane, or mainstream. Another common mistake is the belief that folklore is always false, as people frequently express their disbelief by declaring, "That's just folklore!" Folklore can be completely true, in the sense of portraying actual events or being scientifically accurate, though its "objective" or "scientific" truth or falsity may not be its most important aspect. What may be more important is the "truth" that folklore conveys about the attitudes, fears, and beliefs of a group, which in turn shape and maintain the identity of that group. The rumor that the U.S. government deliberately used the AIDS virus to kill African Americans has no basis in *fact,* but it reflects the *truth* that many African Americans feel their communities are under attack by racist government policies.

Folklore is the unofficial culture of a group, the means by which information and attitudes are transmitted and interpreted within the group. The folk group may be categorized in any number of ways—by nationality, ethnicity, occupation, avocation, family, age, gender—and the group may be any size, numbered in the single digits or the millions, but always the group will share some common core of tradition. In our research, for example, a folk group may be students at a specific university, or even members of a specific athletic team or sorority.

Folklore takes many forms, but whether oral (jokes, stories, songs, jumprope rhymes), customary (blowing out candles on a birthday cake, knocking on wood), or material (stone walls, Easter eggs, matzoh balls), it conveys the collective wisdom—techniques for living, worldview— of the group who share them. The information may be presented clearly, as in proverbs ("Slow and steady wins the race"; "Beer before whiskey, mighty risky; whiskey before beer, have no fear") or cures (cure hiccoughs by eating a teaspoonful of dry sugar or drinking out of the far side of a glass), or in more coded forms such as riddles, jokes, games, and holiday customs.

Folklore is transmitted informally from person to person within a group by aural means and observation, by custom and practice. No one needs formal lessons on when and how to decorate a Christmas tree to know the community's expectations, unless they are new to the community and not steeped in its folklore. Folklore is characterized by both continuity and change. An item's basic form persists through time, but it undergoes constant changes during the transmission process. Folklore is re-created each time it is performed. For example, most of us learn jokes in an informal process by hearing them told. We do not need to memorize a joke in order to repeat it, and when we retell a joke, we use our own words and gestures. Moreover, each time a person tells a joke, it may be told differently, with different words, gestures, emphases, and with sensitivity to context. Certain jokes may be withheld to avoid offending an audience—or told loudly with the opposite purpose in mind. People do not share the same jokes with their peers as with their grandparents, or at the Thanksgiving table as in a bar.

People often misunderstand folklore as being a remnant left from an earlier stage of culture, possibly interesting or picturesque, but without any meaningful purpose. However, folklore always serves a function, whether of education, social control, expression of attitudes and emotions, or strengthening of social bonds. A particular item of folklore will exist only as long as there is some need for it. As a culture's needs change, the item will be adapted to meet those needs, but if need for the item disappears, so will the folklore. Folklore will also adapt to meet changing technologies or times; for example, stories of pets in the clothes dryer have changed to ones about pets in the microwave. We both remember vividly a story that circulated through our junior high school:

There was this girl, one of the hoods, who had a big beehive that she kept heavily hairsprayed. One day in class the guy behind her saw blood trickling down her neck. Then she collapsed. They rushed her to the hospital but she was already dead. When they examined her, the doctors found that spiders had nested in her hair and had eaten into her brain.

This story, told about beehive hairdos in the 1950s and early 1960s, was later told about hippies' long hair in the sixties and dreadlocks in the eighties, but always with the same message about cleanliness and the groups who supposedly did not practice it.

One of the ways in which legends, especially legends dealing with sexuality, change is that they are circulated within increasingly younger groups. Consider these two legends:

A boy and girl are out parking on a dark road. They have the radio on and suddenly there's an announcement that a deranged killer has escaped from the local insane asylum. He can be recognized because one of his hands is a hook. The girl gets really scared and wants to go home. The boy doesn't want to but she keeps insisting, so he slams out of there, driving out really fast. When they get to the girl's house, he goes around the car to open the door for her, and there hanging on the door handle is a hook.

This boy and girl are out parking one night and when they get ready to leave, the car won't start. The guy tells the girl to wait there while he goes for help, to lock all the doors and just stay inside. Well, she begins hearing these scratching sounds and a constant tapping. She gets really scared but all she can do is curl up, cover her ears, and wait. Then it's morning and there's a policeman knocking on the window, telling her to get out, come with him, and not look back. Well, of course, she looks back, and there's her boyfriend hanging by the feet from a branch over the car, with his fingers brushing the roof and his blood dripping on it.

In the 1950s and 1960s, these legends were told mainly among high school students; even in the 1970s, students at Indiana University, some of whom knew the exact bit of road near their various hometowns where the events happened, reported having heard these in high school. An important aspect of these legends, with their strongly implied warnings against parking and becoming sexually active, was that they circulated among teenagers first getting their driver's licenses, with all that entailed of freedom of movement and escape from adult watchful eyes. As one more example of young people maturing earlier these days, the stories have moved over the years into younger groups so that they are now collected from eight-year-olds who heard them as just some more, not too scary, campfire stories. After all, how risqué (risky?) is necking considered these days? How many teenagers wait for the privacy of a car on a dark road to begin exploring sexual activity?

So ever-present in the background of people's lives that it becomes almost invisible, folklore nonetheless shapes people's behavior and reactions to events. A large part of what many of us know about our bodies, in both health and disease, we have learned informally, from kids on the playground or colleagues at work, from piecing together the information contained in folk beliefs, jokes, legends, and personal experience narratives. In matters of sexuality, folklore goes beyond classroom lessons of mechanics to fill in, satisfy, and answer—in piecemeal fashion— all those questions about what people actually do and how they do it. A joke laughed at by a young teenager without understanding, lest the puzzled listener disclose naïveté, can be mulled over in private, pieced together, and collated with other bits of information until an explanation emerges.

Folklore is more pervasive than any number of public service announcements or posters and has a greater weight of authority, coming as it does from the collective wisdom and transmitted as it is on a personal, individual level. Knowledge gleaned from the experience of a roommate's cousin's friend is emotionally more trustworthy than information from a textbook. Unless health and sexuality educators, whether working in the local schools or in the Surgeon General's office, are aware of the folklore circulating, their messages may not be heard and they may misunderstand entirely which concerns must be addressed. Warnings about safer sex and clean needles cannot be heard clearly in an African American community whose legendry assures them that AIDS is the result of genocidal U.S. government experiments in biological warfare (Turner, 1993). Educational messages about rape as a violent and illegal act may be drowned out by high school and college-based legends that suggest that gang-rape is not such a terrible thing—unless the victim is the sister of one of the rapists. Educators should also know about unsafe practices presented first in folk narrative, such as inserting gerbils in the rectum for sexual pleasure, which might be copied by some innocent believing them to be common practices.

Folklore Genres

In this book we will deal primarily with two genres of folklore—folk beliefs and contemporary legends—though we will also include some jokes and personal experience narratives. Even folk beliefs that are not fully believed may be acted on, as anyone will recognize who has searched for a piece of wood on which to knock, picked up a penny for luck, avoided walking under a ladder, or avoided stepping on a crack in the sidewalk. We are used to receiving medical advice informally in the short statements of folk belief: Don't go swimming for an hour after you've eaten; give very sweet tea to a person in shock; exercise to relieve menstrual cramps. Folk beliefs give us advice, wisdom, and warnings that we can fall back on in a world full of uncertainties.

Jokes provide a means for discussing taboo subjects or for expressing socially unacceptable opinions, and may be used to disguise aggression. After all, if someone takes offense, the narrator can always say, "It's just a joke." "Aw, can't you take a joke?" The joketeller and audience may not be able or willing to articulate the meaning behind the joke. Indeed, in many cases it is probably essential that they do not. If the meaning were absolutely clear and evident, people would not be able to use the joke as a socially sanctioned outlet for taboo ideas and subjects. Because jokes are a means of saying what one really thinks without the responsibility attached to actually saying it, they provide a view deep into a group's attitudes and concerns.

Another folklore genre through which people share ideas about sexuality is the personal experience narrative (PEN). PENs are narratives we tell about events in our own lives—not just an oral history or a response to a question, but a developed narrative. These are the stories that we've polished in the telling; if we listen to ourselves, we hear the same phrases and wording we've used before. The story may be brought out whenever the discussion provides the right theme, for example, vacation nightmares, childhood scars, how a couple met. Women often have PENs about their first period, bleeding through at embarrassing moments, the first time they had sex, giving birth. Sometimes, these stories are so good that someone who already knows the story may ask for it: "Tell them about the time that. . . ." Sometimes, other people will start telling the story and it will become an anecdote in general circulation.

Other Health-Related Folklore

In this book, we are concentrating on folklore that deals with sexuality, but health educators should be alert to folklore about drug use and other health-related issues. Drug-related legends include those about the stoned babysitter who roasted the baby and put the chicken in the cradle; the honor student who plucked his eyes from his head when he was tripping; the drug dealers who pass around sheets of LSD-laced decals and PCP-laced temporary tattoos to school children; and the following two examples:

There was this girl who was tripping really hard one time, and she thought she was carrying her brain around in her hands. She kept on staring at it and talking to it for hours and hours. She lived in a dorm, and one of her friends snuck up behind her and yelled "Boo!" She freaked and dropped her brain and has been loco ever since. She's in a mental institute now and just keeps on looking for her brain.

There was this 17-year-old girl who lived in New York City, in this slummy, beat-up apartment building. She was a major druggie, and this was a true story, because the newspapers all had the story in them the next day. Anyway, she took some acid one day and started tripping out; nobody was in the apartment, and she started imagining all kinds of weird stuff. She was looking down at her arms and hands, and she thought she was an orange; her skin looked orange and bumpy and rippled, like an orange peel. Anyway, she went to get a butcher knife, and when they found her the next day, she was lying on the kitchen floor in a pool of blood, with the skin on her arms all peeled and sliced off!!

Whether or not these horrific acid trips ever really happened, the stories can serve as warnings of the dangers of certain psychoactive drugs.

Recently, health-related folklore has begun to surface in a new area that reflects changing fashions: body piercing. In 1998, students began to report such legends as the following:

This story begins that a young girl who just got to college decides to pierce her nipples, and she does. She follows the directions that the piercer gave her to clean them, but they continue to be sore after the healing process should have ended. She continues to clean them daily, but they remain sore, so she returns to the piercer about two months after the initial piercing. The piercer tells her that it takes some people's piercings longer to heal than others, and to just keep cleaning them. Three weeks pass with no change in her condition, but on the fourth week the pain in her nipples begins to spread to her breasts. She endures it for three days, then her nipples begin to harden beyond the norm. She immediately goes to the hospital to be examined, which she is. Unfortunately, she somehow contracted gangrene in her nipples and it spread to her breasts. She was forced to have her breasts removed and replaced with implants. This met with only limited success as the infection had already spread to her heart. She died.

Obviously, this story communicates a clear message about the dangers of piercing and the importance of keeping piercings clean and of following up with medical care if there are any signs of abnormality. The student who reported this story said he had pierced himself, using sterilized equipment, more than twenty times, but the only piercing he maintained was a nipple ring. He said the story gave him reason to clean his piercing every day and to discourage friends from getting nipple rings. There are, of course, risks involved in piercing, including potential infection (Tweeten and Rickman, 1998), and for that reason the Association of Professional Piercers (APP) has established health and safety guidelines for the profession. This is a good example of a legend carrying important warnings about health risks, providing health educators with opportunities to introduce useful and accurate information. As new health risks and health issues, such as body piercing, arise, new folklore will also circulate and old folklore may be modified.

The Collection and Use of Folklore in This Book

The legends and folk beliefs presented in this book were collected by folklore students and by the authors. The cited material reflects a variety of collecting techniques—taperecording, transcribing directly, recreation from notes, student written assignments—but in each case attempts to preserve the original language of the narrator. The folklore students collected from friends and relatives as well as through self-collections (reporting what they had heard in the course of their own lives). Beliefs on reproductive issues were collected through specifically directed studies, but the legends were collected through undirected fieldwork. Material also emerged in class discussions, was collected in interviews with a few knowledgeable volunteers, arose during a conference workshop on the work in progress, and surfaced in many informal interactions. We collected mostly from students at the University of Georgia, but also informally from colleagues, friends, the teenage children of friends, and simply by listening at home and while traveling. This is not a systematic or all-inclusive collection, nor could it be, given all the diverse groups—geographically, racially, religiously, ethnically, by class, sex, and age—comprising the United States. Most of the material was collected from Southern white Christians. There are certainly differences among different cultural groups, born of different worldviews, in their beliefs and fears connected with sexuality and associated behaviors; there is also much held in common. Legends we heard in Australia and England, as well as throughout the United States, were very similar, with only the details such as location changed. Additionally, judging by the legends collected by folklorists in other parts of the country and discussed at conferences, in newsletters and journals, and on the Internet, this is, at least geographically, a representative collection.

It would be impossible to collect all of the pertinent folklore, in part because folklore is constantly changing, both as it is re-created for each individual performance and as it is adjusted to the community's needs. By the time this is in print, new legends will have appeared and others may have dropped out of circulation. There will certainly be new topical jokes—lagging only slightly behind the latest news story.

What Do a Folklorist and a Sexuality Educator Have to Say to Each Other?

At this point, it is important for us to emphasize very clearly some things we are trying to accomplish in this book. Folklorists often feel that their work is marginalized—considered too much the trivia of every day to be "scholarly" and too esoteric to be useful. We have found folklore to be extremely useful in education; unfortunately, educators, who hold many of the misconceptions about folklore we have tried to dispel in this chapter, are often unaware of its applications. Folklorists and sexuality educators need to be talking to each other, just as we have done in conceptualizing, researching, and writing this book. We want this work to be a model of how two seemingly unrelated areas can connect and inform each other. Our goal is to make sexuality educators aware of the value of folklore for understanding the concerns, needs, and fears of their students and the role folklore can play in their teaching practice. We suggest that educators elicit from the students/learners the folklore they already know and use that as a basis for discussions about issues related to sexuality and health. Throughout the book, as we analyze the folklore we have collected, we examine the role it can play in different learning experiences. There are wide ranges of folklore and learning environments, so that an educator will need to decide what is culturally and age-appropriate; the range of folklore provides a great deal of flexibility and options.

The book provides *examples,* not a complete account, of the kinds of folklore that are circulating. These examples are used to stimulate readers to recognize folklore when they hear it and to collect, analyze, and use it. As with all folklore, new material will continue to emerge, so the collector's work is never done. By focusing primarily on one relatively homogenous group (students at one university), we are exploring the range of folklore that may be found within one group that is usually not thought of as a "folk group." While the informants who contributed folklore to this book do not represent the full range of diversity found in the United States, there is some diversity in age, religion, race, ethnicity, sexual orientation, class, place of origin, as would be expected in many groups that at first glance may appear homogenous. We hope this will encourage educators to collect and use folklore no matter what group they are working with. In spite of the relatively limited range of informants, much of the folklore we collected is prevalent throughout the country and is shared by diverse groups.

While an item of folklore always carries its own particular information, its meaning and function are dependent on the context, which includes both broader socioeconomic-historic context and the immediate performance context (the individuals, time, and place). We use folklore in this book as a way of understanding groups' and individuals' current concerns around sexuality. We suggest some of the possibilities of interpretation and some of the issues that have emerged in discussion with our students. You and your students will most likely find others.

The point is to be alert to what folklore is circulating and to be prepared to work with what the students have heard. Remember that even if the narrator dismisses the story, the listener might not. Also remember that even if people pass on a legend as the dumbest thing they have ever heard or as a joke, their very act of transmission shows that there is something about it that intrigues them, that makes them want to share it.

Not all students will know equal amounts of folklore. Just as there are some people who are good joketellers and who always seem to know the latest while others are hopeless at telling a joke and routinely forget the punch line, there are people who are more or less alert to the other genres. Some will claim never to have heard a legend, that their family and friends do not tell that sort of thing. Sometimes, it just takes pointing out a legend they do know for them to recognize that they have indeed heard others. In a recent conversation with family members about this project, several people denied ever having heard folklore or passing it on. However, when we mentioned the stolen kidney story discussed in Chapter 9, they recognized the story, described how they had heard about it, and engaged in a long discussion of its probability, providing a perfect example of how folklore works, even for those who think they are not "folk."

2

CONTRACEPTIVE JELLY ON TOAST AND OTHER UNINTENDED CONSEQUENCES OF SEXUALITY EDUCATION

❑

A doctor reported that he had fitted a 23-year-old woman with a diaphragm. When she returned to the doctor for a check-up, the doctor noticed a purple stain on the center of the diaphragm. When he asked the woman about it, she told him it was a stain from the jelly she used with it. He asked her what brand she was using and she answered, "Smucker's grape jelly."

A first reaction to this story is usually laughter at the punch line, followed by disbelief about this being a "true" story, and amazement that, if it is true, anyone could make such a ridiculous mistake. On one level, many of the stories in this chapter can be read as focusing on the ignorance of the client/patient, but another more useful reading is that the educator/health care practitioner was at fault for presenting information in ways that facilitated misunderstandings. There are many ways, which will be explored throughout this book, in which folklore can help sexuality and health educators in their practice. This chapter focuses on one potential role of folklore—to point out the nature of errors, whether they have actually occurred or not, that can be made in educational processes. The following stories focus on attempts at contraception, so the consequences of the misunderstandings are serious—unplanned pregnancies. While the ungainly attempts are often presented humorously in the story, the results are often devastating for the woman (and man) involved. The opening story and the one following were reported by a student who heard them on her father's AutoDigest tapes of an obstetrics/gynecology conference. It is important to note that even though these stories were collected from a seemingly reliable source, they have all the earmarks of contemporary legends.

> A doctor reported that another woman had been using a diaphragm, but had immediately become pregnant. When he examined the diaphragm, he found the center was cut out. Because there had been no center when she had been fitted for the diaphragm, she cut it out of hers.

A similar story was published in the journal *Hospital Pharmacy* in 1987. A student nurse reported that she had been teaching new mothers about child care and contraception:

> After giving one of the lectures on contraception, a fifteen-year-old, who had received no prenatal care, reacted in astonishment to what I said about how contraceptive jellies should be used. After explaining how the jellies needed to be applied vaginally prior to intercourse, the mother realized for the first time how she had become pregnant. She had purchased a contraceptive jelly from a retail pharmacy and routinely had been placing it on her toast at breakfast! She said that she had received no instruction on how the jelly was supposed to be used and just thought that jellies were for toast—not for intravaginal use. (Cohen, 1987, p. 956)

Although this version was reported in 1987, the story is very persistent and made a big comeback ten years later. A reader wrote to advice columnist Ann Landers (Landers, 1997):

> It seems a woman has filed suit against a small mom-and-pop pharmacy because she purchased a tube of contraceptive jelly, spread it on a piece of toast and ate it. She then had unprotected sex, believing she was "safe" and became pregnant.
>
> The contraceptive came with instructions, but the woman says the pharmacist should have put a specific warning on the box saying it wasn't effective if eaten. She is asking for a half million dollars, even though she is quoted as saying, "Who has time to sit around reading directions these days, especially when you're sexually aroused?"

One contributor to *FoafTale News* reported that this story of oral use of contraceptive jelly was circulating widely in May and June, 1997, through the media and Internet (Hiscock, 1998). The same contributor also reported an e-mail of a first-person narrative by a public health nurse that had been forwarded to him. When a pregnant woman is asked by the nurse about her contraceptive practices, the woman shows the nurse "vaginal foaming pills (about the size of a Necco wafer). She said, 'I've been taking them just like the doctor told me—every time I have sex I take one. They're hard to swallow but I manage'" (Hiscock, 1998, p. 17). Describing the pills as resembling a specific candy does help explain some of the confusion; however, these may be more accurately described as about the size of a thumb joint and about one-half inch thick.

Another story, told as a legend or a joke, relates that a woman became pregnant after the birth control pill kept rolling out of her vagina. This is the reverse of the jelly on toast story, for in this case a woman uses vaginally what should be taken orally. Actually, hormones are well absorbed vaginally, so the vagina could work as a delivery site for birth control pills, though it would certainly not be recommended. A story reportedly told by someone working in a pharmacy also illustrates another misunderstanding of how oral contraceptives work:

> A woman kept coming in to get her birth control pills at a point where she ought to be only halfway through with them. The pharmacy workers finally got suspicious and asked her if she was taking one a day like she was supposed to and she replied, "Yes, and so is my husband."

One student reported watching a documentary on television in which young teenagers discussed sex:

> Some of the girls said they knew of other girls who would steal one birth control pill from a sister's pack. They would take the pill before having sex and think they were protected from becoming pregnant.

There are also similar condom stories. For example, one student reported that after a nurse demonstrated how to put a condom on, using her hand as a model, a couple used it by carefully covering the man's hand. This mistake was discovered after the woman became pregnant. As far as we know there have been no similar mishaps after the popular demonstrations of condom strength and elasticity that involve the educator's pulling a condom on over his or her head.

Rather than focusing on the likelihood that any of these incidents could really have happened or on the lack of understanding by the people involved of reproductive anatomy, health educators should reflect on what these examples say about contraceptive education in clinical and other settings. Many of these stories are examples of what Greenberg (1985) has named "iatrogenic health education disease," the condition in which health education has made learners less healthy. Certainly, health education that results in a woman eating contraceptive jelly and becoming pregnant would fit this definition. In the diaphragm stories, it is clear that careful and thorough explanations, with more realistic assumptions about the common understandings of terms such as jelly, could have prevented these mistakes. A description of the function of the spermicidal jelly would have made it clear both that grape jelly would be ineffective and that the jelly would need to be placed vaginally or in the diaphragm, not on toast. Even a brief explanation of the way a diaphragm works would have prevented a woman from assuming that a fitting ring was the model for an effective contraceptive. One of the clear messages sexuality educators should get from these stories is that education about contraceptives needs to be specific, concrete, and as literal as possible. If a woman were actually handed a tube of spermicide, shown how to apply it to a diaphragm (not a fitting ring), and helped to insert it vaginally (in a class, this can be done on a plastic model, though in clinical settings, the woman should get a chance to insert it in herself to gain assurance that it is in correctly), it is unlikely that any of the above errors could be made. An explanation of how to use the vaginal tablet, rather than "Use one just before sex," would be much more effective. Because these are sold over the counter, however, a purchaser would not have to see a health care practitioner, who might give some instructions and explanation. As the Ann Landers story points out, people do not always read instructions, due to low literacy, not being able to read English, too small print, assuming they know what to do, or just being in a hurry. Most people would agree that the purported lawsuit against the pharmacy is inappropriate, but it is a strong reminder to pharmacists about their potential role in health education. Explanations of how oral contraceptives work in a woman's body should certainly keep anyone from assuming that a man should take them along with his partner or that a woman should just take one before intercourse. While a model of a penis is not necessary for a condom demonstration, it is important to note that the banana, or whatever item is used, does represent a penis. Even if the previous examples are rare or even totally apocryphal, other problems could be prevented by this concrete approach. For example, a demonstration may prevent the mishap of applying so much spermicide that the compressed diaphragm flies out of the woman's fingers. In all areas of health and sexuality education, the same rules apply: be specific and concrete, with appropriate visuals and hands-on demonstrations.

Language is also very important. For example, for some people the term "contraceptive" is so closely associated with oral contraceptives (the Pill) that referring to any contraceptive may connote oral use, a meaning reinforced by such terms as jelly, cream, and tablet. Another story, recounted by a folklorist, while clearly in the joke genre, also reveals an important point about language:

> By the way, I recall from my adolescent years a story about condoms. A couple wishing to avoid pregnancy was told by their doctor to use them. A few months later they returned and told the doctor that pregnancy had occurred even though they had used condoms. When the doctor asked, "Did you follow the directions on the package?" the husband replied, "It said 'place on organ,' but we don't have an organ so we put them on the piano."

This joke/story probably served as a means for young adolescent boys to check out their own and others' knowledge about condoms and "organs," but it is unlikely to have been accepted as a true story. However, it is a reminder that we can never make assumptions about the vocabulary of learners, either their knowledge of technical terms or their use of certain slang or euphemisms. It is important to make sure everyone is talking about the same thing. Often health educators will ask students to list all the words they can think of for penis or vagina or other relevant terms. Once the list is generated, they can then suggest that everyone use the same specific term (usually the correct medical or anatomical term, but in some cases it may work better to use the most common slang term). In any case, it would be clear what an individual meant when using a certain term. If an educator is unclear about what a slang word means, it is better to ask than to try to appear cool and knowledgeable, while actually being wrong. For example, in parts of the

South, *cock* refers to female rather than male genitalia (Cassidy, 1985). Slang terms are very specific culturally and historically. By using the term "cool" above, we were assuming a certain common understanding of a term that, in fact, may be very out of fashion with certain age groups or meaningless for certain cultural groups. It is better to ask them to clarify a term or to say, "I think it means this but I'm not sure, so let me know if I'm wrong." They will.

Health care practitioners who complain about "noncompliance" may be neglecting their own failures to provide the kind of information that would help someone follow through on a prescription or recommendation. By collecting folklore such as these legends and using them to analyze failures of educational practice, health educators may create much more effective communication.

3

YOU CAN'T GET PREGNANT YOUR VERY FIRST TIME

Understandings of Fertility and Birth Control in Folk Beliefs

❏

Avoiding Pregnancy

"If you do it while standing up, gravity will keep the sperm from reaching its destination."

"If you douche right after it will wash away all the sperm."

A clear presentation of facts is important in sexuality education, but unless the shared and often unspoken beliefs such as those above are dealt with directly, the facts are mere abstractions that don't contradict deeply held misunderstandings. An educator can discuss the ovulatory cycle and issues around pregnancy and contraception in great detail, but still leave whole areas of students' beliefs untouched. The following beliefs were collected by college students, as part of folklore class assignments, from informants representing a wide range of ages. Students collected folklore about both how to prevent pregnancy and ways in which pregnancy can happen. Not surprisingly, men reported mostly on the former and women on the latter. Men may wish to assure women that it is safe to have intercourse, even using misinformation as lines to persuade women to "go all the way," while women may have anxieties about a variety of ways in which pregnancy might occur.

According to this collection of folklore, a woman *cannot* get pregnant if/when:

she has intercourse standing up.

she has intercourse in a hot tub, in water, or in the shower.

she has intercourse on top.

she has intercourse for the first time.

she only has sex a few times.

she holds her breath when the man comes.

she does *not* have an orgasm.

she douches with any of the following: a commercial preparation, ice water, vinegar, Coca-Cola, 7-Up, 5-Alive (the latter two reportedly work before or after intercourse).

she drinks Coca-Cola immediately after intercourse.

she jumps up and down following intercourse.

she stands on her head following intercourse.

she takes a long, hot bath immediately.

she urinates after intercourse.

she sneezes after sex.

the man drinks alcohol before intercourse.

she has intercourse during her period.

he withdraws before ejaculation.

she is breast-feeding.

he uses Saran Wrap or a baggie as a condom.

she is raped.

These beliefs may be held by middle school, high school, and college students, and even by adults beyond college age. If a sexuality educator discusses the physiology of the menstrual cycle and reproduction in great detail but never explains clearly that a woman can get pregnant standing up or the first time she has intercourse, the erroneous beliefs can co-exist with the detailed scientific information.

One simple exercise in a health or sexuality class is to elicit from students in a brainstorming session, or assign them to collect, as many beliefs as they can about preventing pregnancy; this should not place them in the awkward position of admitting their own acceptance of certain folk beliefs. Students can then apply the information they have learned in the class to evaluate these beliefs. They can discuss the fact that douching with any substance may wash out or kill some sperm but also may force some sperm closer to and through the cervix. This is a perfect opportunity to discuss other issues related to douching, such as the research that suggests it increases the risk of ectopic pregnancies, probably by forcing microorganisms up through the cervix, thereby causing reproductive tract infections that can lead to tubal scarring and ectopic pregnancies. The connection in terms of mechanism should then make even more sense. They also might discuss why contraceptive potential has been wrongly attributed to different beverages (colas, the most frequently cited choice for douching, have been reported to have a weak spermicidal effect *in vitro,* that is, "in glass").

The explanation provided by one student informant for the contraceptive effects of the man drinking alcohol is that the sperm become "drunk" and cannot swim straight. There are a number of issues that can be raised in discussing this belief, in addition to explaining that alcohol won't make sperm too drunk to reach their destination. For example, heavy or even moderate alcohol consumption by women may reduce their fertility (Jensen et al., 1998). However, if this information is given, it is important to make it clear first of all that drinking will not work as a method of birth control and that long-term regular alcohol consumption is not the same as hoping that a binge of alcohol consumption one evening will result in successful contraception. It also should be noted that continued drinking after pregnancy could result in fetal alcohol syndrome. It would also be useful to discuss the effects of alcohol on sexual activity, such as the associations between alcohol and sexual assault, and between alcohol and "unsafe" sexual activity. This could also lead into a discussion of a common double standard related to drinking and sexual activity. It is often considered socially acceptable for a man to be sexually active after drinking heavily, but a woman is often blamed for being so drunk that she unintentionally becomes sexually involved. This double standard is also extended to sexual assault, so that being drunk becomes a mitigating factor for a man who is charged with sexual assault, while a woman who has been sexually assaulted is blamed for "allowing" the assault to happen because she was drunk.

There also may be a discussion of some beliefs as either good or harmful practices *unrelated* to pregnancy. For example, urinating after intercourse may reduce risk of urinary tract infections, by washing bacteria out of the urethra before they can ascend into the bladder. If an individual had once heard that it is a good idea to urinate after intercourse, but not why, the obvious assumption might be that it prevents pregnancy. While activities that increase intra-abdominal pressure— coughing, sneezing, bearing down—will force some semen out of the vagina, especially within a few minutes after ejaculation, these are hardly reliable forms of birth control. The belief about urination may reveal a basic misunderstanding of anatomy, as some young women have described the urine as washing away the sperm. Adolescents are often unaware that in women there are two completely separate passages—the urethra and the vagina. Given that many girls think there is only one "hole," a combined vaginal and urethral opening, this is not surprising. It is easy to imagine that if someone assumes urine travels out the same passage that sperm enter, then urination would, of course, seem a good way to wash out the sperm. With boys there is the reverse problem in understanding anatomy; because sperm and urine do both exit the penis through the urethra, boys are often confused about the connections between ejaculate and urine, and fear that they may accidentally urinate while having intercourse. These gaps in basic anatomical knowledge indicate the need for teaching anatomy in upper elementary school and middle school. Even though some sexuality education is negatively labeled as "plumbing classes," this information is essential since many adolescents simply don't know how the internal "plumbing" relates to the external fixtures. Even college students are generally very hazy on male anatomy and cannot label parts on a diagram or explain the roles of most of the internal structures (vas deferens, prostate, etc.).

Unfortunately, sometimes these mistaken beliefs can help shape or justify policy. The false belief that a woman cannot get pregnant by rape—allegedly the reproductive system stops working under stress—was used by a politician in a debate on eliminating state funding for abortion. Henry Aldridge, a Republican legislator in North Carolina, explained that women don't get pregnant from rape because "the juices don't flow, the body functions don't work" (*Chicago Tribune*, 1995, p. 4). There is no physiological basis at all for this argument and there is plenty of contradictory evidence. The ancient false belief that if a woman does not have an orgasm, she cannot get pregnant reinforces the false belief about rape. If it were true that a woman's lack of an orgasm would prevent pregnancy, then, based on reports of adolescent women's sexual experiences, there should be a lot fewer teenage pregnancies! And certainly there are many adult women who have become pregnant without benefit of orgasm. It is also important to note, especially to prevent the "victim-blaming" that often accompanies rape, that a woman may have an orgasm when raped but this does not mean she enjoyed or welcomed the rape—only that a physiological response beyond her control occurred.

A lot of women believe that breast-feeding prevents pregnancy and have relied on lactation as a primary method of birth control. There is a complex relationship between breast-feeding and fertility. The hormone prolactin, which is produced during lactation, can inhibit ovulation. Some cases of infertility are due to excess levels of prolactin in nonlactating women. The frequency with which a woman breast-feeds helps determine the level of prolactin; frequent feeding results in higher prolactin which can prevent ovulation. However, eventually ovulation will occur, especially as feeding becomes less frequent. One problem is that a woman may wait for menstruation as a sign that her cycle has begun again before she resumes use of contraceptives. However, ovulation precedes menstruation and, if she has had unprotected intercourse while waiting until she menstruates again, the next period she sees may be after her next birth. On a population level, regular, frequent breast-feeding may be effective in spacing pregnancies. However, no individual should rely on it to prevent pregnancy.

Previous research has examined some of these "myths" among teenagers as part of larger studies. (Although "myth," like folklore, is commonly used to label a falsely held belief, its technical meaning for folklorists is quite different. Myth tells about events in the remote past and explains how the world came to be the way it is, accounting for or justifying some aspect of the current world, whether physical, behavioral, or moral. In this book we use myth in quotation marks to designate the popular, rather than technical, meaning.) For example, in the oft-cited study by Zelnik and Kantner (1979), over half the teenage women surveyed who had failed to use contraception during intercourse said they did so because they thought they could not get pregnant. The most frequent reasons given were that they were too young, that they only had infrequent intercourse, because of "the time of the month," or unspecified. In a survey of teenagers, Ostrov and co-workers (Ostrov et al., 1985) found that many teenagers believed that a woman could only become pregnant "if she wants to" and could *not* become pregnant the first time she had intercourse. In Kisker's (1985) research using focus groups of teenagers, it was reported that many "myths" were common, including not getting pregnant the first time of intercourse or if intercourse is infrequent. While this research clearly points out the prevalence and seriousness of those "myths," it does not really offer a thorough and comprehensive examination of all the misinformation found in folklore. The work in the classroom to identify these beliefs needs to be ongoing, in order to keep in touch with beliefs that may change over time and within different groups, and to be aware of the range of misinformation. It is also important to examine these beliefs for their possible influence on behavior and to note how folklore is used to justify behavior, such as a woman not using contraception because she only has infrequent intercourse.

Getting Pregnant

While some students may cherish folk beliefs that offer them an unjustified sense of safety from pregnancy, others may be frightened by beliefs about how easy it is to get pregnant. For example, these beliefs were collected by college students (mostly women), again from a wide range of age groups, about how a woman can get pregnant:

kissing
sitting on a boy's lap
from a toilet seat
going to the bathroom after a boy
from a swimming pool or a hot tub
swimming in a pool with a boy
touching too close in wet bathing suits
kissing a boy in your bathing suit in the rain
dancing too close to a boy
sperm getting on your legs
sperm touching you *anywhere*
lying on top of a boy while naked
rubbing genitals together while wearing underwear
only during the girl's period
from oral sex

It is important to note that these beliefs may coexist with contradictory ones. For example, having intercourse, either in a hot tub or in water is identified by some informants as a way of preventing pregnancy, while others consider swimming pools and wet bathing suits to be dangerous transmitters of sperm. Some of these beliefs have also surfaced as contemporary legends. For example, a student reported that, when her family was having a backyard pool installed, her friends warned her about the risk. They said a girl in Alabama had become pregnant swimming in a public pool after a boy had masturbated in the water. Another reported that a couple had been "fooling around" in a hot tub and the man ejaculated into the water. As the student described it, "the sperm swam through the water and eventually made its way to impregnate the woman." In one of her newspaper columns, Ann Landers addressed the issues of pregnancy without intercourse, with at least one letter presenting the hot tub story as a personal true story. The expertise of the well-known columnist helps validate the "truth" of the story. Health educators may also add to the validity of these stories; according to one student, her ninth grade health education teacher had told them the following story as fact:

> A teenage couple were "parking" and making out. They both got practically naked, wearing only their underwear. The male, being a randy 17-year-old, reached orgasm as they were pressed against each other and the girl got pregnant. The neat-o thing was that she was still a virgin!

If young people really hold these beliefs, they can live in unreasonable fear of toilets and swimming pools, but may simultaneously believe themselves safe in much riskier situations. Many of these beliefs can be viewed in the context of overwrought textbook descriptions, which have been analyzed by Martin (1991, p. 490), of active, energetic sperm on a "mission" to fertilize the egg while undertaking a "perilous journey." By the time the stories of the long uphill swim of the heroic sperm—through a potentially hostile vaginal environment and cervical mucus, to the final sprint at the end to be the one to fertilize—have been told, it is not surprising that these athletic sperm are seen as able to swim across a pool, jump between wet bathing suits, or wiggle across the body from any point where it is deposited to find the vaginal opening. It is not hard to believe that they can even live on toilet seats awaiting a chance to latch on to a woman's skin and crawl toward her vagina. One student reported that she had heard stories of girls who had gotten pregnant after giving a "hand job" to a boy and then using that hand to wipe themselves after urinating. In much of the folklore, once within the body, sperm become even stronger; one student reported that she had heard that sperm can "stay active" up to six months in a woman's body. Research indicates sperm can live in the vagina no longer than six hours and, protected within the crypts (small pits or recesses) of the cervix, may survive at the longest for seven days.

In Georgia, many students are very familiar with Civil War stories, which are considered part of a shared heritage. One of the most dramatic stories of sperm hardiness was reported by several students about a Civil War soldier who was shot in the scrotum. The bullet passed through him and, covered with sperm, penetrated the abdomen of a woman, who then became pregnant. One version reports that they later got married and had more children, with the sperm produced by his remaining good testis.

Another story also warned of the dangers of inanimate objects carrying sperm:

> When I was in the eighth grade, a friend of mine told me about a woman who had gotten pregnant by a tomato. The story was that an old tomato picker ejaculated on a stack of tomatoes that were directly shipped to the market. An older woman somehow fell into the tomatoes. For some reason the woman was not wearing underwear, and a tomato carrying the picker's sperm was lodged into the woman—thus making her pregnant.

These beliefs about sperm hardiness and persistence may have been fostered by health educators. In the efforts by educators to undo the belief that coitus interruptus is effective as birth control, they/we often discuss the millions of sperm in the small drop that is released just prior to ejaculation. (Discussing the difficulty in controlling ejaculation is not effective in education, because that control becomes a point of pride; the warning about a high sperm count in the pre-ejaculatory drop may work, however, partly because it reinforces a young man's sense of his own potency.) Educators should also discuss the risks of ejaculation on the vulva without penetration. Unfortunately, these risks may be amplified in students' minds so that they do not recognize that ejaculation on other parts of the body, such as the hand, may be an alternative that is both safe and satisfying. In a sense, the attempt to counter the dangers of reliance on ineffective approaches to contraception may lead to unreasonable fears. This may be considered another symptom of "iatrogenic health education disease," in which health education has created fears so that low- or no-risk activities are considered high risk, perhaps leading to someone avoiding a low-risk activity and substituting a high-risk one.

Another commonly expressed false belief—that a woman can *only* become pregnant while menstruating (contradicting another false belief that a woman *never* can get pregnant if she has intercourse while menstruating)—probably results from one of the ways menstruation is first discussed with young girls. Menstruation is often described as meaning "you can get pregnant and have babies now." The person making such a statement is often trying both to explain that menstruation is an indication that physiologically the reproductive system is maturing *and* to convey something of the responsibilities that accompany that maturation—both that a young woman is able physiologically to become pregnant and that she should protect herself from that possibility. However, the statement may be heard much more literally and specifically as "the time at which you menstruate is the time at which you can become pregnant." One student reported the story of a girl who thought that her first period actually meant she was pregnant. Another college student, who was a very high academic achiever, explained that the first

33

time she had intercourse in high school, she had planned it midway between menstrual periods to reduce the risk of pregnancy. When it was explained to her that it probably would have been safer during menstruation, she was very surprised (and relieved that no pregnancy had resulted). Similarly, folklore students reported the beliefs that "a girl can always know one absolutely safe time between menstrual periods when she cannot get pregnant" and that "when you have your period, it is to protect the egg in you." In Kisker's (1985) study of teenagers, the majority did not know when the most fertile phase of a woman's menstrual cycle is likely to occur. Through our experience teaching at the college level, we have observed that few students have developed a clear grasp of the menstrual/ovulatory cycle, even if they have completed a high school sexuality education class.

The woman who "protected" herself by having intercourse midway in the cycle also held a common misunderstanding about the importance of "midway," though she had reversed "safest" and least safe times for unprotected intercourse. Many adults firmly believe that halfway between menstrual periods is the time of ovulation, when, in fact, ovulation occurs approximately 14 days *before* menstruation no matter how long or short the menstrual cycle. The error arises from the common practice in puberty education and sexuality education of using a 28-day cycle as the standard. Students then learn that ovulation occurs on day 14 and, unless they are specifically and repeatedly told the correct information, they interpret day 14 in one of two ways: (1) ovulation always occurs on day 14 of the cycle, no matter how long it is; or (2) ovulation always occurs halfway through the cycle. An easy way to approach this in the classroom is to ask on what day a woman is likely to ovulate if she regularly has a 34-day cycle (or any length other than 28). Usually, the majority of students answer day 14 or day 17, illustrating the two interpretations above. Very few correctly answer day 20, and the ones that do have usually taken the woman's health course on campus. Surprisingly, Zelnik and Kantner (1979) reported that 64 percent of teenagers who said "time of the month" was their protection against pregnancy correctly knew the time of greatest risk. It would be interesting to know whether that was a general time (i.e., ovulation) or specific as to when ovulation is likely to occur in different cycles. Based on college students' knowledge, the former is more likely. Possible consequences of misunderstanding when ovulation occurs are unintended pregnancies because of reliance on the wrong "safer" times or difficulty becoming pregnant when timing intercourse to the wrong days in the cycle. One student reported the belief that the "fastest way to get pregnant is to have sex every night for a week, 14 days after the last period." One drawback of this approach is that a high frequency of ejaculation reduces the sperm count in men and can decrease the chances of pregnancy in marginally fertile couples. This is also not likely to work on a shorter cycle, such as a 26-day cycle, which is not uncommon. Educators should forget the 28-day cycle. Principles of the cycle can be discussed (such as time from menstruation to ovulation is variable, but ovulation to menstruation is usually 13–15 days), giving a *range* of cycle lengths, and then having women volunteer to chart their own. Anonymous data can then be shared with the class and analyzed.

Confusion also arises from the use of the terms "safe" or "safer" in sexuality education. Before AIDS became a major health issue, the term "safe" in relationship to sexual activity meant that pregnancy could not occur, as in the statement "there are no safe times of the month." "Safer" times of the menstrual cycle are times in which there is less risk of pregnancy. Education about HIV/AIDS uses the term "safe sex" or more accurately "safer sex" to define activity in which the risk of transmission of HIV is greatly reduced. Those terms may also be used to include other sexually transmitted diseases. It is essential that an educator clarify what kind of "safety" is under discussion and to explain the mechanisms by which risk is reduced. In addition, because a condom reduces risk of pregnancy and HIV transmission, that dual function may be ascribed to other methods of birth control even though oral contraceptives, Norplant, and DepoProvera will not hinder viral transmission. On the other hand, students also may assume that spermicides kill only sperm, when, in fact, they can kill certain microorganisms that cause sexually transmitted diseases. While spermicides reduce transmission of gonorrhea and chlamydia, they have not been shown to decrease HIV infection.

Fertility/Infertility

Are folk beliefs ever scientifically right? Many folk beliefs have at least some kernel of truth and many have a good scientific basis. For example, here are three beliefs reported about infertility treatments:

Dealing with men: Tight jeans can cause impotence and even infertility.

I have heard that infertility specialists say that in order to get pregnant they shouldn't have sex often so that the sperm level in the man's semen can increase. The more often a man ejaculates, the less viable sperm is in each "batch" of ejaculate.

Do not get out of bed for at least 30 minutes after intercourse if you want to get pregnant.

In terms of the first belief listed, while there is no evidence that tight jeans cause impotence, it is well documented that if the scrotal temperature gets too high, sperm count decreases. Anything that would hold the scrotum close to the body would increase the temperature, so recommendations to men with low sperm counts include wearing boxers instead of jockey shorts, wearing loose trousers rather than tight jeans, not riding bicycles, and spraying the scrotum with cold water. Another recommendation is to avoid hot tubs or long hot baths, advice which may then contribute to the belief that pregnancy cannot occur in a hot tub. However, it is not a brief immersion in a hot tub that causes low sperm count but repeated exposures over a period of time. In addition, what may be a factor in reducing fertility in borderline situations can certainly not be relied on as a contraceptive method. Wearing jockey shorts and tight jeans is not a substitute for using a condom as a birth control method.

Many couples eager for a pregnancy do have intercourse too frequently, which may lead to reduced sperm count and reduced chance of pregnancy in situations in which fertility is marginal, so the advice to reduce frequency of intercourse to enhance fertility may be useful. However, this should not be extrapolated to reach the conclusion that the best way to *prevent* pregnancy is to have frequent intercourse.

The last belief above is also correct. If a woman lies on her back after intercourse for 30 minutes, the cervix, which has been pulled up with the rest of the uterus during arousal, will then descend back to its original position where it will rest in the semen that has pooled in the posterior fornix (the upper part of the vagina behind the cervix). This will make it easier for the sperm to ascend through the cervical os (opening of the cervix) into the uterus. If the woman is resting with her hips raised on a pillow, this also increases the chances the sperm will get to the os. The same rationale supports the missionary position (traditional man on top position) as one that may enhance the chances of conception; however, the belief that "if you stand on your head after intercourse, it will be easier to conceive" seems to be pushing the idea too far and would be rather difficult for less athletic women! As with the other advice about fertility, the reverse does not provide good birth control. A related belief about preventing pregnancy is that a woman will not get pregnant if she is on top. While being on top may not be the best position for a woman who wants to get pregnant, it certainly is not an effective approach to birth control. Along the same lines, while jumping up and down after intercourse would be a bad idea for a woman trying to get pregnant, this activity is not recommended for contraception. Therefore, even if folk beliefs (or scientific information) are correct, it is crucial to point out the problems of extrapolation into other areas.

There are also beliefs about the effects of certain products on fertility. The false belief that drinking the soft drink Mountain Dew can lower sperm count has been reported by a number of students. This belief has circulated widely enough that a Planned Parenthood speaker wrote in to "Dear Abby," asking the columnist to help correct this misinformation because some young people were relying on drinking Mountain Dew as a contraceptive. The letter writer felt that in her experience, this was the "myth" that was one of the most "potentially dangerous" and "difficult to dispel" (Van Buren, 2000). One student, apparently recognizing that a little humor might be appreciated by the professor, wrote on his folklore exam:

> I was simultaneously writing this final and slimming my chances of fatherhood as I enjoyed a refreshing 12-oz can of Mountain Dew at the outset of this exam. I have long heard that Yellow-5 (the least abundant ingredient in Mountain Dew, and also found in various other sodas and candies) kills sperm, shrinks your testicles, or causes sterility. It seems that the testicle shrinking is the most popular of the above three, but being as how I can not understand how a soda can affect the size of a bodily organ, I always say that it just kills sperm.

Since douching with various soft drinks is often believed to prevent pregnancy, it is not a large step to identifying drinking specific beverages as a means to prevent a man from being fertile. However, it is Yellow-5 that is identified as the active factor, obviously very powerful even though it is the "least abundant ingredient," rather than any factor common to soft drinks. A woman student reported that a male friend of hers had sorted through a package of Starburst candies, removing all the yellow ones and offering them to her, saying, "You want these? I don't want them, they have Yellow-5." The student noted, "And everyone knows that Yellow-5 supposedly shrinks a man's testicles and penis." A number of rumors have identified other products as affecting fertility. For example, Turner (1993) reported on warnings that circulated in New York in African American communities in the early 1990s about a drink called Tropical Fantasy: "The reason? Apparently the KKK owned the company, and the tasty beverages contained a secret ingredient that sterilized black male drinkers" (p. 103). There was no truth to this rumor, but that certainly did not stop this story from circulating and being at least half-believed.

In discussions of issues around infertility, there is often confusion about sterility and impotence, also known as erectile dysfunction. Because the testes produce both sperm and testosterone, a hormone that plays an important role in the sexual response, the two are linked inappropriately. One reason many men do not opt for vasectomy is the baseless fear that the surgery, which cuts a tube that carries sperm from the testes, will also result in a loss of erectile function. The careful definition of terms and explanation of function can help reduce such fears and misconceptions.

Aphrodisiacs

This girl was out on a date and the guy gave her some Spanish fly so that she'd be more receptive to his advances. He left her alone in the car for a few minutes and when he came back, he found she'd gotten so horny while he was gone that she'd impaled herself on the gear shift.

Long before Viagra, there were stories and rumors about substances that would cause sexual arousal and enhance sexual performance. There are a wide variety of beliefs about these alleged aphrodisiacal substances that will enhance sex drive and potency. Some suggestions are repeatedly collected: oysters, ginseng, Spanish fly, green M&Ms, strawberries (with whipped cream or chocolate, according to one source), chocolate, Tequila or the Tequila worm, wine (or any kind of alcohol), Ecstasy. Other alleged stimulants of libido are much rarer in collections. One student reported that snails are an aphrodisiac and another noted that burning vanilla candles is "a sexual stimulation to both sexes and it could increase potency." Oysters appear in most collections and there are bumper stickers with slogans such as "Eat oysters and love longer." The association between oysters and potency in males may be partly due to the shape of oysters, which is similar to that of testicles. "Prairie oysters" and "Rocky Mountain oysters" are terms used to refer to cooked animal testes. In a similar association between shape and function, the worm found in the bottom of bottles of mescal (Tequila worm) is also associated with potency, though this belief is extended to include the Tequila itself. However, using alcohol can have negative effects, because it can increase arousal but reduce a man's ability to have an erection. One student listed saltpeter, which is interesting because saltpeter has exactly the opposite effect—to dampen any sexual drive. M&Ms of different colors have been ascribed with various powers and it is unclear why the green ones would be linked with libido. However, as with the Mountain Dew story, it is common for a particular product to be identified with specific risks and functions that have little to do with the actual ingredients.

One informant listed pheromones, an interesting variant, because there is a great deal of research on pheromones as sexual attractants in animals. Pheromones are hormone-like substances that are released from one individual and can bind to receptors on other individuals, carrying chemical messages. For example, it has been postulated that the phenomenon of menstrual synchrony (a group of women living in close proximity all having their menstrual cycles fairly closely synchronized) is caused by pheromones released from one woman and picked up by another. This is an area of research that is still active, so this belief may be correct—at least in some animal species. However, it is unlikely that pheromones will be available soon as an aftershave or perfume, even though certain scents, such as those using musk, are marketed with the idea that they may be sexual stimulants.

Another informant mentioned Ecstasy as a drug that has aphrodisiacal effects. Ecstasy, a "designer" drug, is in the category of hallucinogens. It can create euphoria and hallucinations, as well as serious adverse reactions such as paranoia and acute panic (Boston Women's Health Book Collective, 1998). One legend involves a girl who overdoses on Ecstasy at a party and then undresses and masturbates in front of everyone. This legend validates the belief that Ecstasy is a sexual stimulant, though it is also, as with many other drug stories, a warning against the consequences of using it. There are other warning stories about overdoses of aphrodisiacs that often end with the man suffering from priapism, a condition in which his penis remains painfully erect no matter what he does. While many of the alleged aphrodisiacs, such as oysters, are harmless, others, such as Ecstasy, carry a large risk. Spanish fly (powdered Spanish beetle, *Lytta vesicatoria*), which is given great credence in legends, has no proven aphrodisiacal powers and would not cause a woman to become so "horny" she would use a gear shift as a dildo. It does cause an irritation of the urinary tract which may be mistaken for arousal, and it can be lethal in high doses (Taberner, 1985). Viagra, an extremely popular drug for treating erectile dysfunction (or ED, as a previously untouchable topic has become a subject of mainstream media and advertising), carries some real risks, and men with heart disease have been warned not to use it. The predominant folklore about the new drug has not been in the category of legends but of jokes, many of which allude to erections:

> Did you hear that six cases of Viagra were stolen from a dock in San Francisco? They're looking for a gang of hardened criminals.

It will be interesting to see if Viagra legends appear and, if so, what form they will take.

Paying Attention to Beliefs

Though many informants presented the beliefs in this chapter as false, there often seems to be some lingering doubt. In a situation in which a young couple is eager to proceed with their love-making, the false comfort from the half-believed ideas that it's safe because it's the first time, because they don't do it very often, or because it's her "safe" time, may be enough to keep them from worrying—at the moment. It is important then that these beliefs, elicited directly from the students, be addressed in sexuality education classes so that students get some clear answers about what's safe, what works and what does not, rather than relying on folklore passed on through a peer or a persuasive lover.

4

LESBIANS DON'T HAVE PERIODS AND OTHER MENSTRUAL FOLKLORE

❏

Many young women have their first formal education about menstruation in elementary or middle school as part of puberty education. This may range from a short one-time session, perhaps featuring a video produced by a manufacturer of "feminine hygiene" products (the term itself indicates that menstruation is seen as unclean), to much more comprehensive programs integrated into the curriculum throughout the year. The classes are sometimes for girls only, to reduce the risk of giggling and to increase the likelihood that the students will feel comfortable asking questions. Sometimes the classes are co-educational, where changes during puberty for both males and females are discussed openly. There are wide variations in how explicit these classes are; for example, girls leave some classes still wondering where the tampon actually goes, not having quite worked out the separation of the urethral opening from the vaginal opening. Sometimes the class is taught by a school nurse; even though the nurse may be an excellent teacher, the message is that the topic is one that requires an expert—your own regular teacher can't deal with it either because it is too technical or too sensitive. The decisions about who teaches, including the gender of the teacher, whether the class is co-ed or not, and how the topic is approached all have effects on how the material is perceived by the students. One recommendation is that a man and woman team teach and, in order to model the comfort the students should have in dealing with these issues, she should field questions about nocturnal emissions and erections while he responds to questions about tampons and menstrual flow. (It should be noted that there is usually a double standard in puberty education: Boys learn about issues related to sexuality—wet dreams and erections—while girls learn about issues related to reproduction, that is, focusing on the menstrual cycle.)

Unfortunately, many girls may have begun to menstruate before they get to take a class, which means that they have to face their first period (menarche) with only informal knowledge, from peers, older sisters, mothers. The film *Carrie* contains one of the most dramatic fictional representations of a girl beginning menstruation without information. When Carrie begins her period in the shower after gym class, she panics because she thinks she is bleeding to death. In response, her sadistic classmates pelt her with sanitary napkins. While most girls don't have such traumatic experiences (and don't proceed to destroy their school and kill classmates in response), many have had negative and embarrassing experiences because of lack of timely information. Just as it is problematic in terms of health education to assume that the "average" menstrual cycle is 28 days, it is also inappropriate to focus only on the average age of first menses, given that there is a wide range of normal starting ages. Girls who started menstruating in fifth grade complain that elementary schools don't have pad and tampon vending machines in the girls' bathrooms. It also should be noted that technically menarche, the first menstrual period, signals the completion of puberty, which means that puberty education about changes in the body is likely to occur well after many changes have been noticed. Boys are even less likely to receive puberty education that helps them understand menstruation, and they may be even more embarrassed to ask their questions. While a parent may sit down with a boy and explain the changes he will experience during puberty, changes that girls experience, especially menstruation, are unlikely to be part of that discussion. Knowledge boys share with their peers about menstruation is generally conveyed in the form of jokes, which can serve as tests of who is clued in enough to "get it" and also who can be the "grossest" (see the jokes later in this chapter), but also leave the less informed the difficult task of sifting through to find the information they need. If a measure of men's comfort with menstruation is their willingness to buy menstrual products and/or their understanding of the differences among these products, then most young men would fail these tests.

Whether or not they have formal education, young women often depend on beliefs about menstruation for advice and warnings. For example, these are some beliefs women and adolescent girls reported they had heard when they were around the age of menarche or slightly older:

To postpone your period for a week or so, you should take a lot of baths.

You shouldn't bathe when menstruating.

Menstruating women should bathe more often than normal.

Your period stops when you are immersed in water.

Menstruating women shouldn't swim or sit in hot tubs because the flow of blood will stop and be unhealthy for the woman.

When you swim if you have your period, you won't bleed in the water.

If you have sex during your period, it will damage you internally and you will never be able to bear children.

If you have sex while you're having your period, the boy will get a yeast infection.

Sex during menstruation is dirty and causes diseases.

A woman can't feel any pleasure if she has sex while she's menstruating.

Don't go outside barefoot when you have your period.

If you eat red foods, your period will be heavier.

Don't eat chocolate or sugar or drink carbonated beverages (cramps won't be so hard).

Don't drink too much acid when you have your period.

Having sex will stop cramps or make them better.

Exercise is good for cramps.

Don't wet your hair while you have your period (it will make your cramps worse or it will make your neck pop).

Drinking cranberry juice will reduce cramps.

As is common with a collection of beliefs, several are contradictory. For example, there is both the advice not to have sex and the advice that sex will reduce cramps. Bathing and swimming are common subjects. For many years, health educators, particularly when doing puberty education, tried to counter the common belief that a woman shouldn't bathe or wash her hair while menstruating. Apparently, these beliefs still persist to some extent, but clearly these repeated messages have had some effect, as in the advice that women should bathe more often than normally. This emphasis on bathing during menstruation may also be related to concepts of women as innately unclean (see Chapter 7). The relationship between water and menstruation as expressed in beliefs varies. Baths are identified as a way to delay menstruation, which is surprising since another set of folk beliefs suggests that a hot bath will bring on menstruation and, in fact, is believed by some to be able to induce a miscarriage if the water is very hot. The first belief in the list above implies that there is something positive about delaying menstruation since it is presented as a means to achieve postponement. Attempts to change the onset of menses may be to keep it from interfering with a social event, such as a date, or a vacation. On the other hand, many young women learn that there is no problem with swimming during menstruation because menstruation stops when a woman is in the water. There is no physiological basis for that belief but it still persists and, of course, even if it were true, many would find it a problem getting to and from the pool. Perhaps the theory underlying this belief is that the water pressure would keep the blood from leaving the vagina, or perhaps even from leaving the uterus through the cervix. The prohibition against swimming, bathing, or washing hair may be related to the idea that getting chilled during menstruation is unhealthy. For example, one African American student reported that her grandmother claimed that the reason white women are so sickly is that they don't wear enough clothes during their periods; her grandmother also insisted that women should keep their shoes on during menstruation. The idea of keeping heavily clothed and shod seems to give counter warnings to the idea of bathing often.

Several beliefs state that delaying menses is bad because it is unhealthy. This may be related to the belief that menstrual flow contains toxins and that menstruation is a way to cleanse those poisons from the body. Menstrual blood is seen as "dirty" blood, whereas there is actually nothing wrong with it. The menstrual flow is primarily endometrial (lining of the uterus) tissue and blood that was supporting that tissue as it became thicker during the cycle. If the egg is not fertilized, the hormonal support for the endometrium is withdrawn, the blood vessels constrict and rupture, and the endometrial tissue is sloughed off. If fertilization had occurred, the endometrium would have continued to grow and the developing embryo would have burrowed into it and become implanted. Menstruation has many meanings for women. For example, to women trying to achieve pregnancy, menses is a "failure," while to those trying to avoid pregnancy, the flow brings a sigh of relief. However, it is interesting to examine why menstruation would be seen as toxic. For women who are not necessarily concerned about pregnancy, menstrual flow may be seen as an indication that the body is functioning well. When that attitude is combined with the feeling of renewed health which accompanies the onset of menses due to relief from various premenstrual changes (such as water retention and breast tenderness), a delayed flow may be perceived as "unhealthy," retaining what should be released. Margie Profet proposed a very controversial theory, discredited by many scientists, that menstruation plays an important role in flushing out potential disease-causing organisms (Travis, 1997). This theory implies that if the blood does not flow, the body is not cleansed.

The relationship between sexual activity and menstruation is also a recurring theme in these beliefs. There are general statements that sex during menstruation will damage women internally, and that it is dirty and causes diseases, with the more specific note that men can get yeast infections that way. With more information about blood-borne diseases such as AIDS, menstrual blood could seem even more threatening. It would be much more risky for someone to have sexual contact with a woman who is HIV positive if she were menstruating at the time, because the virus is found in high concentrations in the blood.

A great deal has been written in recent years about views on menstruation cross-culturally. Delaney, Lupton, and Toth (1988) examined many cultural issues related to menstruation, including taboos around sex:

> But the blood of the menstruating woman is somehow dangerous, magical, and apparently not something he wants to get on his penis. It is thus necessary to protect the penis from menses.
>
> Although the menstruating woman is still considered to be magical, the primary reason for the dread of intercourse during menstruation appears to be the blood itself, which has associations in the male mind with pain, death, battle, injury, and castration. It has been found in those cultures where the intercourse taboo is most strictly enforced, there is a significant degree of castration anxiety (fear of losing the penis) among the males. But official explanations for the intercourse taboo range from the holy to the hygienic, and they do not acknowledge that the male is afraid of *anything*. (Pp. 18–19)

Many cultures and religions have specific taboos about sexual activity during menstruation. For example, Orthodox Jewish law prohibits a man from even touching a woman during menstruation and she must be cleansed through the use of the mikvah, a ritual bath, before there can be any sexual activity. In addition to protecting the male from any alleged uncleanliness, this prohibition also increases the linkage of sexual activity to procreation, because, while intercourse during menstruation should not be relied on for contraception, it does greatly reduce the possibility of fertilization occurring. Therefore, the time during which intercourse is permissible includes the time of greatest fertility. The additional warning that women can't feel any sexual pleasure during menstruation is another way to limit women's sexual activity during that time, though, interestingly, many women report heightened sexual arousal premenstrually and during menstruation. In writing about health beliefs in rural Jamaica, Sobo (1997) interprets menstrual taboos as less about men's fears than about ways of controlling women's sexuality:

> Men are the strongest supporters of menstrual taboos. These taboos include a ban on sex as well as on cooking. The ban on sex is used for, among other things, controlling female sexuality. It discourages women from sexual expression, while at the same time and in combination with the idea that menstruants are unclean, it encourages women to feel shame about their genitals. (P. 156)

In addition to beliefs about sex during menstruation, a great deal of attention is given to foods that should be avoided or increased during menstruation. Meat is believed to increase flow, an outcome that is usually considered to be negative. However, another belief is that eating red meat will help replace the lost blood, and this belief does have some scientific basis in the fact that meat is a good source of iron, which is lost during menstruation and is necessary in the formation of red blood cells. However, it may be the association of the color of the meat with the color of blood that is more important in making this advice seem logical than is the knowledge of the composition of hemoglobin. Other foods are said to increase cramps and common recommendations advise to avoid carbonated beverages and salt. One of the beliefs above is that cranberry juice reduces cramps. It may come from confusion about the reason for the common advice to drink cranberry juice, which is to reduce the risk of urinary tract infections such as cystitis. Cranberry juice does contain a substance that keeps bacteria from binding to the bladder and thereby causing infection. In a similar confusion of beliefs, in the previous chapter there was a discussion of the incorrect belief that urination after sex could prevent pregnancy, whereas it actually is a good way to prevent bladder infections. To avoid cases of iatrogenic health education disease, educators need to spell out the purpose for which a recommendation is made, not just issue a statement, for example, that it's good for women to drink cranberry juice.

There are also jokes, primarily told by men, related to food and menstruation, of course drawing on the color similarities with blood:

Q. What's grosser than gross?
A. Your sister gives you a glass of tomato juice . . .with a pubic hair in it.

Q. What's grosser than gross?
A. Eating a cherry popsickle and finding out your sister puts her used tampons in the freezer.

Another relationship between food and menstrual blood came up in a discussion with African American women high school students:

If you don't want your man to go anywhere, put your period blood in his spaghetti. But you can't tell him, you got to put it there and not say anything.

While the other young women in the group reacted with disbelief and disgust, a few had heard of this, and one added:

Some of the boys know, and to this day, they will not eat nothing red, like drink Kool-Aid, or eat spaghetti; they will not eat it if you made it, especially if you make it.

One agreed:

I cooked spaghetti the other day and . . . I asked my boyfriend, "Want some?" and he said, "Nope, I'll wait till I get home."

A discussion with a different group of African American girls from the same area yielded a similar discussion:

INTERVIEWER: See, last period, all the boys were like, "I don't believe in it," but they kept telling me more . . . and they were like, "If a girl cooks spaghetti, I won't eat it."

STUDENT #1: I heard that one. They won't eat nothin' red. Tomatoes and rice . . .

STUDENT #2: Why?

STUDENT #1: 'Cause you know . . . girls put their period blood in it.

STUDENT #2: Oh, okay.

STUDENT #1: 'Cause my mama's boyfriend sure enough don't eat hers. Nothin' red.

STUDENT #3 (later in conversation, returning to this issue): This was on a movie, but this had happened. This lady, she cooked her husband this meal, and she put her cycle in it, and it like made him . . . he was always dogging her out, but then she put her cycle in the spaghetti, and he started . . . it's like he started treating her better and stuff. . . . it was disgusting!

INTERVIEWER: Everyone says, "I've never done it, but I know someone who has . . ."

STUDENT #3: I don't know nobody who has done something like that. That's nasty. Think about it. You don't want nobody doing your food like that!

STUDENT #2: That's why, I mean you got some men who will, but true men will not eat spaghetti.

STUDENT #1: Then my grandma told me some men will not eat chocolate cake.

STUDENT #3: You can put it in there, too. It's brown or whatever, you can't really tell. So a lot of men won't eat chocolate cake.

Since women traditionally have been the ones who prepare food, they have the opportunity to put in "extra" ingredients. In this case, the ingredient is not meant to harm but to control through the magical power of menstrual blood. In other cases, it could be meant to harm (ground glass, poison), to control (abused woman putting tranquilizers in her husband's food), or as an unseen gesture of defiance at the more powerful (numerous stories of commercial kitchen workers and servers spitting in the food of customers who have treated them badly).

Although this set of beliefs about the power of menstrual blood was new to us, we soon discovered it referred to in another source. Sobo (1997) wrote about the concept of "tying" in rural Jamaica:

Substances that transport toxins out of the body (e.g., sweat, urine) can cause sickness simply because they are dirty with waste. They can also be used to control the minds of others whose bodies they enter. Women, as a way to tie men to them and thus secure men's love and money, can use their menstrual blood in cooking. Veronica told me that her cousin's friend collected her menstrual blood for this purpose by squatting over a steaming pot (hot steam helps gravity to ease out some of the menses). Sometimes, used menstrual rags or pads are soaked in water to loosen the blood, which is then squeezed or wrung out of them and added to food.

The food most commonly used in tying is *rice-and-peas,* a reddish-brown dish made of rice, coconut milk, and red beans. A woman can steam herself directly over the pot as her rice and peas are cooking. Red pea soup, stewpeas, and potato pudding are also known as potential menses carriers. All are the correct color and commonly eaten. (P. 154)

It is quite possible that the girls who reported similar beliefs were from Afro-Caribbean families, or the shared beliefs about tying through menstrual blood may have come from common ancestral sources.

Tampons

There are many beliefs specifically about tampons:

Using tampons takes away virginity.

Tampons will make you no longer a virgin or will loosen you up.

Using a tampon will block the flow so it makes cramps worse.

A woman can't wear tampons until she's married.

Only sluts use tampons.

If you sleep with a tampon in, it will suck your womb and vaginal canal completely dry.

If a lesbian uses super or super-plus tampons, it means she's been with men.

Don't wear tampons because you can get sick, lose it inside of you, and it's very painful.

Many of these beliefs relate to sexuality, primarily by indirect reference to the effects on the hymen and on vaginal "size." The hymen is often seen in folklore as a major barrier to penetration, rather than what it actually is, which is a thin membrane that comes in many shapes and sizes, usually only partially covering the vaginal opening rather than blocking it. Many girls won't even have much of an identifiable hymen by the time they reach menses, and it is very rare that a hymen would block tampon use. The beliefs that a woman can't use a tampon until she is married or that only sluts use them or that a tampon will cause loss of virginity rely on the idea that the hymen remains a barrier until there is active penetration, either by a penis or a tampon. The names of the smaller tampons—"Juniors" or "Slenders"—are meant to correct that impression by making it clear that a virgin can still use them.

In addition to the effect on the hymen, there are also obvious references to changes in the vagina, with the idea that a tampon "will loosen you up," which implies stretching the vagina in some way. The belief about lesbians and tampon use (provided by a lesbian) also implies that vaginal size and capacity depend on how much penetration there has been. In Chapter 7, we discuss folkloric views of the vagina as either a tube of varying sizes in different women or an endless space that can swallow up objects—including large numbers of tampons that "disappear" or "get stuck." Neither intercourse nor use of super plus tampons will change the capacity of the vagina. On the issue of tampons "sucking dry" the uterus and vaginal canal, tampons will absorb vaginal secretions as well as menstrual blood. However, they would have to be located within the cervical os, rather than the vagina, in order to wick anything out of the cervix. They do not have such a powerful wicking effect that they can draw fluids through the narrow opening of the cervical os and, if they could, it is not clear what would be "sucked" out of the uterus.

There are also reports about additional advice around tampon use:

Don't leave a tampon in too long.
I was told not to leave a tampon overnight because of TSS.
Be careful—you can lose the tampon string up there.

Some of this useful advice can be seen as evidence of good health education. Toxic shock syndrome, also known as TSS, is a serious and sometimes fatal disease caused by toxins produced by the bacterium *Staphylococcus aureus*. Using highly absorbent tampons which are left in for long periods of time seems to increase bacterial growth and toxin production. A concerted campaign to explain how to reduce risk of TSS, along with changes in tampon labeling (and removal of certain tampons from the market), have made the occurrence of TSS much rarer. Young women in their teens and early twenties are at particular risk, so it is good that the health education message is reaching adolescents. The attention to the risk of TSS associated with tampons may have helped stimulate the rumors, spread both orally and by Internet, about other alleged dangers of tampons: that manufacturers add asbestos to tampons to promote more bleeding in order to sell more products; that tampons contain toxic amounts of dioxin; that rayon in tampons causes TSS, as well as ulcerations of vaginal tissue. Accurate information about the allegations in these rumors can be found through the website for the Food and Drug Administration at www.fda.gov. On the last item, it is true that occasionally tampon strings do get pushed far inside the vagina, making removal more difficult. However, these mishaps do not make tampons impossible to retrieve; perhaps this warning is given because of the fear or discomfort many young women experience at the thought of actually reaching inside their own vaginas, as a string pushed inside would necessitate. Stories of lost tampons are explored further in Chapter 7.

There are, of course, numerous jokes about tampons and objects used for that function:

Q. How do vampires use tampons?
A. As teabags.

Q. How do vampires use the string on a tampon?
A. As dental floss.

Q. What does an elephant use for a tampon?
A. A sheep.

Q. What does it mean when you come home to find a nickel on
   your dresser and your mattress is missing?
A. Your elephant's got her period.

Of course some of these jokes are specifically used to insult specific groups:

Q. How can you tell if a [fill in ethnic group] woman is having her period?

A. She's only wearing one sock.

Legends and Personal Narratives of Embarrassment

Menstruation provides many opportunities for embarrassment stories, including legends and personal experience narratives. Several of these embarrassment stories focus on cheerleaders, who are also discussed in Chapters 6 and 7. Fine (1992) describes the cheerleader:

> The cheerleader is generally seen both as a symbol of virtuous young womanhood and, because of her position, as a highly desirable sexual possession, who wears sexy clothing and dances in an enticing fashion. (Pp. 59–60)

Legends of cheerleaders' menstrual embarrassments may serve to make them seem less superior to the young women who have not achieved this status and to the young men who see them as desirable sex objects:

> A cheerleader was doing one of those splits where two others hold her up in the air. Just then her period started and she started bleeding through the white underpants/shorts that cheerleaders wear.

> Another cheerleader could tell her period was starting but wasn't prepared so she wadded up some toilet paper, but the end of the toilet paper was sticking out her underpants when she went up in one of these in-the-air splits.

> Another cheerleader was in one of those in-the-air splits, when her maxi pad fell out and hit the girl underneath, who was so startled that she dropped her.

56

While these stories bring cheerleaders down to the level of girls who bleed like any other, there are also narratives of very ordinary women who experience analogous horrors, as in this set of stories reported by one young woman.

> They were all at the beach together and they decided to go to McDonald's. The girl was like when you first get your period you don't really know what to do, you're like, "Can I go to the pool? Can I do this? Am I allowed to go over here?" I mean, you know, "how am I supposed to do this?" And so apparently she couldn't wear tampons or anything and so she was wearing a pad at the beach. She got in the water, everything was fine and she got out, you know, everything was fine, and they went to McDonald's and she just had like a T-shirt on over her bathing suit and stuff and, um, she was at McDonald's, she had flip flops on and her, um, pad fell out and, um, she kind of—this little kid was like, "Mommy, what's that?" and she just kind of like put her foot over it. She goes, "That's mine" and she just walked out with it and left. She was like, "I'm sorry, that's mine." Oh gosh, every time, I swear I just bust out laughing. I mean, it's hilarious.

> Well, actually I heard this one. There's this girl I played soccer with, and um she's like, "You're not going to believe what happened to me. I was like in the bathroom and there was like this mother and daughter in there" and she's like um, "So I was changing my pad and everything, and then like it dropped on the floor, and the little kid was like 'What is that thing on the floor?'" and then um the girl was like, she just kind of stopped and waited till they left, you know. She just kind of said she was so mortified 'cause she didn't want—her Mom was just kind of, her mom gave her the explanation, "Well, honey, I think it's, someone dropped their tissue; I think someone had a bloody nose or something." So um she said she was just mortified and

she didn't come out of the bathroom till someone else had come in and then gone out.

Stories similar to these commonly circulate among girls and women at all-female gatherings, from slumber parties to bridal showers to feminist support groups. Each of the subjects of the stories, which are often first-person narratives, had at the time of the story recently started menstruating, and was still unfamiliar with all the details of maintaining pads in place. The location can be any public area, with many of the stories focusing on sports events, in which the combination of the physical activity and the skimpiness of the uniform creates a less stable environment for menstrual pads. In addition, sports events are highly public and the individual and the errant pad have little protection from viewers on the tennis court or the track or the softball diamond.

Whether the stories focus on a dropped pad or making a mess by bleeding, the crucial issue is the revelation of the fact that a girl menstruates:

> There was a girl and I used to be friends when I was in middle school. . . . Betty was in the other math class and I was in this one and I heard all this commotion going on and she kept like um yelling for me, "Come here, help me," you know, and anyway, she's in the bathroom crying and I'm, I was like "What in the world is going on?" There's this girl named Jeannie. . . . Betty had like leaked all over the seat and just completely blood, I guess, all over the seat and so Jeannie was in there cleaning it all up and I went in the bathroom and she was so mortified, I mean, she was so upset, 'cause I mean like now everybody knows. You're trying to keep it a secret, you know. . . you want all of your girl friends to know, but you don't want the guys to know that you've started or whatever. And then, so I went in there and this teacher, she came in there and then she goes, "Honey, you need to use those pads, you gotta use the ones

that I use, this big"—and they were this big—I mean they were huge, they were like 3 inches wide. And she was like, Betty, she looked at it and she was like, "Nooo way." She was just, it made her cry even more. She didn't come back to school for about a week though 'cause she was so upset.

While many would see the teacher's response as supportive and caring, the girl just sees it as one more person aware of her humiliation. In addition, although the teacher is affirming female solidarity around the problems of a heavy flow, the girl probably does not want to see herself as part of the adult world of women who wear "huge" pads.

One student informant analyzed the stories that focus on the secret of a girl's menstruating state being revealed:

It was just like the only thing, when you're that young, it was, it was like, when you did get your period it was like you're dirty or something. You didn't want the guys to think you were sexually active even though that's not what it meant. It was just like you didn't want them to think you were a slut or something or that's why it started or whatever. Because we were still unsure why it was happening to us and so they were even more unsure of why, you know, this was going on, so you seemed so innocent if you still hadn't gotten your period.

This commentary by the young woman is very telling, as she points out how menstruating becomes equated with being sexually active. A girl who has matured early physically is often identified as "loose" or a "slut." In the days before adhesive pads, vending machines in girls'/women's bathrooms dispensed menstrual pads with two safety pins (to attach the pad to the underpants) in a cellophane wrapper. If someone noticed a girl had those two wrapped safety pins, it was as embarrassing as having a tampon roll out of a purse. The very fact that a girl is menstruating is the embarrassing issue because she is then identified as sexual. The title of this chapter, "Lesbians Don't Menstruate," a belief one student reported, supports the idea that menstruation is associated with hetero-sexual activity; a lesbian is seen as not being a "real" woman because she does not have sex with men and, therefore, also does not menstruate. In an interesting gender difference, in general girls who mature earlier than classmates tend to be uncomfortable with their status and may be picked on and teased about their breasts. However, early maturing boys seem to feel less discomfort. A boy who shaves earlier than his classmates may also develop a reputation as being sexually active, but the double stan-dard works for him because he is identified as a stud; there is no nega-tive heterosexual men's term equivalent to "slut" to describe a man. It is also interesting to note that no students brought in personal experience narratives about embarrassing situations involving wet dreams (think-ing it was urine, washing the sheets before anyone saw) or erections at inopportune moments, such as when standing in front of the class doing a presentation, though these stories certainly exist.

Because menstrual cycles are often irregular in adolescents and be-cause teenagers may be less aware of signs of impending menstruation, stories of unexpected bleeding and the use of unsuitable forms of pro-tection (wadded up toilet paper, Kleenex, even leaves, are common). For example, this story was told by a young man:

> I am from the Pacific Northwest, an extremely damp and "mossy" place. When I was a freshman in high school, I heard of a late-blooming young woman who was out on a date with her boyfriend. Unexpectedly, she started having her first pe-riod. She did not want the young man to find out (they were making out in a car in the woods). So, she excused herself and found a piece of moss, which she used as a surrogate tampon. However, what she didn't realize was that there was a wood tick in the moss. To this day, she has never had a period.

While this could either be a legend or a joke, it depends on the read-ers'/listeners' knowledge that ticks feed on blood. For anyone who has seen an engorged tick, the idea of one swollen with countless periods' worth of blood is completely grotesque. (Actually, a female tick only feeds once and eventually drops off its host after it becomes engorged, in order to lay eggs.)

On the other end of the menstrual continuum, there are many personal experience narratives and legends about the heavy and unpredictable menstrual flows that often occur as women approach menopause. The narratives may involve how much "sanitary protection" is needed during a heavy flow (for example, reporting using a super plus tampon with two pairs of underpants, each with a maxipad with wings) or embarrassing moments:

Leaking through while teaching a large class

Leaking through while a keynote speaker at a conference

Leaving a large bloody spot on a chair at a restaurant

Ruining the sheets (and mattress cover) in a hotel

Leaving a blood stain on a light-colored couch at someone else's house

Soaking a leg cast so thoroughly, it needed to be removed and replaced

For women with heavy menstrual flows, sharing these experiences creates a sense of support and the realization that "I'm not the only one."

Menstruation and Wild Animals

In addition to the dangers of public embarrassment, women are told that when menstruating we also face the danger of attack from wild animals:

I remember being told that all animals could sense when a woman was menstruating, and were drawn to her scent. This was often followed by a story about a couple who went to a cabin in the mountains for the weekend. The woman had just begun to menstruate, and a bear from the nearby woods sensed it. The bear spent the whole weekend trying to get into the cabin.

The camping/bear or beach/shark stories I remember circulating also around [the age of] fifteen. You couldn't go camping because bears could smell the blood and eat you alive. It was the same story for swimming in the ocean except it was a shark. I also believed these stories.

One man, with obvious disbelief, reported seeing a newspaper article about bears attacking menstruating women and his own amused surprise that his wife believed it. As seen even in the informants' reactions, this folk belief and the legends encapsulating it are not as readily dismissed as some other beliefs. It is an interesting enough question that there was an analysis of the issue of whether bears are attracted by human menses in the alt.folklore.urban newsgroup (Kelly, 1994). The author did an analysis of bear attack data and concluded that menstruation is not a factor. She also cited a study that actually tested the theory that black bears are attracted to menstrual odors (Rogers, Wilker, and Scott, 1991). Running a series of experiments, the authors found that bears are much more interested in garbage and in tampons soaked in beef fat than in menses-soaked tampons. The black bears also showed no particular interest in menstruating women who were in close proximity for extended lengths of time. The authors point out that much of the concern about menstrual odors and bears "became widespread when 2 menstruating women were killed by grizzly bears (*Ursus horribilis*) in Glacier National Park in 1967, prompting government agencies to circulate brochures warning menstruating women against entering bear country" (p. 632). They also note that another author has concluded that there was no evidence that menstruation was a factor in grizzly bear attacks, but also that one study suggested polar bears find menstrual blood attractive.

There may be some basis of truth in the beliefs and legends that persist for sharks because sharks are attracted to blood, so menstrual blood could have the same effect if leaked into the water. However, the warnings about bears do not include that they are attracted to the blood from a wounded person or animal. The belief about bears may rely on the belief that menstrual blood is different than other blood and is dangerous or even magical, or it may have to do with the connection of menstruation to sexuality. People also tell stories of dogs sniffing the crotch of a menstruating woman or humping her leg. In Australia, one story is that male kangaroos will be sexually attracted to menstruating women. These beliefs and stories serve to present women and their sexuality as "animal-like."

Avoiding Misunderstandings about Menstruation

When young women were asked to discuss what they had heard about menstruation as teenagers, they reported some basic misunderstandings, which could clearly lead to very negative feelings about the onset of menses:

> I just remember not knowing about it—like I thought you had to wear a pad or tampon every day, for the rest of your life, not just 3–7 days a month.

> Since I refused to really talk to my mom about it, I thought you had to wear a pad every day for the rest of your life.

The way menstruation is first explained to girls could easily cause this misunderstanding—that once you start you will menstruate until you are around 50. That may stick in their minds more than the statements that it happens once a month. It is also common to believe that menstruation is like urination or defecation, in that there is a feeling that "you have to menstruate," at which point the woman excuses herself to go to the bathroom to put on a pad or insert a tampon. One of the problems is that in much of puberty education, the basic physiological and physical changes are described—growth of pubic and armpit hair, breast development, changes in fat distribution—but the explicit details about the actual experience of menstruation are not discussed. For example, a student may learn that the average flow is 30 to 80 milliliters or even how many tablespoons that is, but it does not mean much. Demonstrations with menstrual products and colored liquids (they don't need to be red) might give a better idea of how much is lost and how much a pad or a tampon can absorb. As with the suggested demonstrations for a diaphragm, a tampon should be inserted into a plastic model, rather than relying on line drawings. Tampons and pads can be passed around in class. The variability in what is considered "normal" in terms of cycle length, length of time of flow, and amount of flow should all be discussed.

Question Boxes, Folklore, and Puberty Education

One of the most important steps a teacher can take in puberty education or sexuality education is to find out the students' concerns and questions. Many do this through a question box, in which students can anonymously write their questions, which will then be answered by the teacher in class. Those who have experience with question boxes have learned a few basic rules. Don't answer the questions until you have had time to look them over; great embarrassment has resulted from just reaching in and pulling out a question to read. There is no need to read the questions verbatim because the misuse of terms can cause a lot of laughter, which will affect even an anonymous writer; questions can be combined ("many of you asked about . . .") and answered in that form. Anyone who has seen a class of adolescents is aware of the wide range of physical development and maturity. Examining questions from a given grade gives an idea of the similar range of innocence and sophistication in one class. Questions may reveal some very basic misunderstandings, while others may show a strong grasp of a complex issue. Below are some question box questions, with the original spelling and punctuation, collected by a teacher from fourth, fifth, and sixth grade students (Scott, 1995):

> Can a guy go to the bathroom and have an erection at the same time?
>
> When you go to the bathroom and you had sex and would you see eggs?
>
> What happens if the penis gets stuck in the vagina and it won't come out?
>
> Wher's the penus on the skelaton? Is the skelaton a boy or a girl?
>
> What happens to the sperm that doesn't make it to the egg?
>
> If the egg in the mother's body doesn't get fertilized does the baby still come out normal?
>
> I already matured but I didn't have my period. Is that usual or am I gifted?
>
> How could you have your peared if you are not married?
>
> What would you do if you were stranded in the middle of the desert and you were having your period and no Tampacks?
>
> What is masturbating: please answer.
>
> Do you have to have cubec hair to make love.
>
> Why do some people have sex more than one time?
>
> What happens if you fall in love with somebody who has aids?
>
> How can you tell when your done having sexs.
>
> What is the difference between homosaipien and homosexual. (Pp. 66–102)

This is a small but representative sample of the kinds of questions teachers receive. Students want explanations of some very basic issues, which may be neglected in the average sexuality education class. They want clear explanations and practical answers. They also often ask questions that are difficult to answer, either because they deal with issues the teacher would be reluctant to discuss at that grade level, because it is hard to know what the student is really asking, or because the questions are simply difficult to answer. For example, what would be the best answer to the question of how you know when you're done having sex or what do you do if you fall in love with someone who has AIDS? The author of the thesis that contains these questions has tried to provide practical advice on how to answer some of the difficult questions.

Given the folklore we have discussed in this chapter, adding another dimension to the question box may be useful. In addition to asking specific questions, students can be encouraged to write down what they have heard about the topic, without having to decide if there is a question to be extracted from a belief or a joke or a story. The teacher can then combine these with questions to explore some issues that students have raised. A belief provided anonymously by one student may stimulate others to remember and contribute beliefs they have heard, without their having to indicate their lack of knowledge by formulating a question; that is, they can state what they heard without having to ask if it's true or not. As with the use of beliefs in the previous chapter, this provides an opportunity for the class to work together to determine what may be true and why, even if it isn't true, there may be some value in it.

5

THE TINY GIFT-WRAPPED COFFIN

Addressing Fears of AIDS

❑

There was this girl vacationing over Spring break in Florida. She met some guy, and they fell in love. They did everything together, and, by the final night of vacation, she conceded to sleeping with him.

The next day, as he saw her off (she had to go back to her college), he gave her a small gift-wrapped box and told her not to open it until she got back to school.

She got back, eagerly unwrapped it, and sat, numbly reading the inscription on the miniature coffin: "Welcome to the wonderful world of AIDS . . ."

This short version of a popular and chilling legend was reported by a man who had heard it in high school, told about a friend of a friend. Many variants exist, including another with a man as the protagonist, which circulated widely before the coffin variant appeared. When the story is told about a man, he is usually out of town on business and picks up an attractive woman at a bar. In the morning she is gone, having left scrawled on the mirror in lipstick, "Welcome to the wonderful world of

AIDS." There are obvious and significant differences in these variants which relate to the gender of the victim, but a key point is that the message is received by a heterosexual man or woman, soon after having had intercourse with a new partner, a previous stranger, for the first time. In most cases where the woman is the "victim," the infecting partner is attractive, romantic, perhaps "exotic," and usually from an entirely different geographic location. There is an intense but brief courtship. In contrast to these variants, with a man as the "victim" there is no apparent romance or courtship. In the stories focusing on women, especially those told by women, there is a very romantic stage of flowers and dinners and no pressure to have intercourse. It is this courtship, this "falling in love," that makes it permissible for her to be sexual with a stranger. One reason teenage women often give for not using contraception when they have had intercourse is that they were carried away by the moment. To be swept away by romance makes intercourse acceptable. The vacation romance in these stories sets up such a "moment," the last night of an idyllic vacation, at which time a young woman might do what she would normally not consider acceptable. The following example, told by a woman to her college student daughter, who was preparing for a summer study trip to Italy, illustrates the use of this legend to warn against the dangers of such romance:

> One year a group of friends decided to make the most of their senior year. Since none of the girls had traveled alone before, they decided to take a summer vacation when school was out. It would only be the three of them since they were independent now.
>
> June came quickly and the girls packed their bags for the Caribbean. They had the time of their lives on the beach, exploring the open shopping market, and enjoying the night life of the clubs. The second day after the girls arrived, a man not older than 22 approached one of the girls. Lynn was having trouble communicating in the open market. Lorenzo helped

her haggle for her price. He spoke perfect English, but from his physical appearance, he was clearly Hispanic. He offered to show Lynn and her friends the island sights. They eagerly accepted. Every day Lorenzo greeted Lynn and her friends. They snorkeled one day, shopped another, tried out the night life; it was something new every time they met. However, each day without fail Lorenzo greeted Lynn with a special gift. She was thrilled; it was a dream come true. No one had ever given her such attention. He took her to romantic dinners every night, and always followed it with a moonlit walk on the beach. Lynn was in heaven. She couldn't believe they had to go home in one short week. The last evening Lorenzo planned an extra special dinner for Lynn. Everything was perfect. He cooked dinner for her in his apartment. She saw no reason why she shouldn't have sex with him; after all, he had made her trip so memorable for her, the least she could do for him was this. Everything was perfect for her first time; she didn't regret a thing she had done. It was a perfect end to a perfect week.

The last day Lorenzo drove the girls to the airport. He gave to Lynn a last gift. She was so excited, but he made her promise not to open the gift until she was on the plane and on her way home. She consented to his request. The minute the plane took off she opened the box. When she opened it she saw a tiny black coffin. An inscription read, "Welcome to the wonderful world of AIDS."

In a number of the stories, the young woman expects an engagement ring; in some the gift is a ring box, with a note inside. No matter which version, there is romance and attraction, or even love. The mother who told this story to her daughter was giving a clear warning about the dangers of men, no matter how attractive and romantic, and, because the daughter was going to Italy, the foreign locale also was very important in the warning aspects of this legend. There is also a racist subtext because the emphasis is on the fact that, even though Lorenzo speaks perfect English, "from his physical appearance, he is clearly Hispanic." This may also play on the stereotype of the ideal Latin lover. Compare this version told by a woman to the same basic story told by a man at the beginning of the chapter and to a typical male-victim narrative:

> This guy went on Spring break down to Florida and he met this really beautiful lady in a bar. And they went back to his hotel room. When he woke up in the morning, she was gone but scrawled across the mirror in red lipstick was the message, "Welcome to the wonderful world of AIDS."

Comparison of these tales highlights the gender difference in the importance of romance in sexual encounters, both according to the narrator's gender and the female versus male "ideal" vacation encounter—romance versus the one-night stand. It is also worth noting that the infecting woman is described entirely in terms of her appearance (beautiful) while the infecting man is described in terms both of being attractive and behaving in romantic, thoughtful, attentive ways. These differences may be taken as cultural gender norms of what women and men want in sexual relationships.

In her book based on extensive interviews with teenage women about sex and romance, Sharon Thompson (1995) discusses the "victims of love," those young women whose romantic beliefs have led to sexual consent. She refers to the culture of romance among young women, including the reading of romance novels and the sharing of romantic daydreams:

> They do this, in part, because romances fulfill a need that's just too hard to satisfy in real life. Teenage girls themselves say they love the novels because they teach about "romance and dating" and allow them to "escape." The place they escape to is the land of romance—a place where girls wait for love and get it and

boys love the girls who want them before and after a pair has
intercourse. . . . (P. 44)

These AIDS stories sharply undermine such romantic views. They say
romance leads to intercourse which leads to AIDS and abandonment;
they say romance is used only to get sex and that sex can be used to destroy. Educators and students need to be able to examine together the
romantic views that govern some young women's responses, views that
can lead to dangerous results, not just within the world of legends:

> And there's another problem, one with serious ramifications
> for sexual education. Although love makes girls and women
> more likely to prevent pregnancy, it makes them less wary of
> sexually transmitted infections, because they commonly as-
> sume, as most people do, that love is the best guarantee of safe
> monogamy. (Thompson, 1995, p. 46)

The "Welcome to the wonderful world of AIDS" legends contain both
truths and inaccuracies about AIDS, but they always express fears about
the risks of contracting AIDS. One of the very important messages in
these stories is that *heterosexual* intercourse can transmit AIDS. Because,
early in the AIDS epidemic, the misdirected emphasis was on "risk
groups," rather than "risky behaviors," heterosexuals often felt a false
sense of security in relationship to the disease. The "Welcome to the
wonderful world of AIDS" stories of heterosexual transmission of HIV
represent a chink in this protective emotional armor, which allows for
the recognition that heterosexuality cannot in itself offer protection. At
a discussion of these legends at a conference, an HIV educator pointed
out that the "shadow side" she sees in young women is a fear of sex and
even romance. Some young women she counseled said they wanted to
give up sex completely.

A second point is the recognition that *one* "unsafe" contact can transmit the virus and cause infection. This is a crucial message to convey,

even though it is also important to emphasize that increasing the number of unprotected contacts with an infected person increases the risk. It is often difficult for students to accept the fact that monogamous but unprotected intercourse with an infected person puts them at more risk than "one night stands" with a number of partners, even with the odds that some are infected. For many, the word monogamy equals safety, and health/sexuality educators contribute to that misunderstanding by not emphasizing that monogamy is protective only if both partners are uninfected and stay that way. To some people, especially adolescents and young adults, monogamy means being faithful to your partner of the moment, even if that partner changes every few months or weeks. It is unlikely that this "serial monogamy" will result in relationships with great trust and knowledge about a partner, but may very well lead to a false sense of security. In examining self-sabotaging logic in terms of HIV/AIDS prevention, Sobo (1995) cites Bolton's (1992) discussion of the problems that occur when monogamy is promoted by health educators as a strategy that is seen as an alternative to safer sex practices. Bolton's research suggests that the vague advice "to know your partner," together with the idealization of monogamy, may result in the large number of women who are not infected by casual sex partners but instead by their long-term partners. For this reason, Bolton recommends that no antipromiscuity messages should appear in AIDS instructional material. An addition to this argument about the dangers of antipromiscuity messages is that an individual may believe that (as with false beliefs about pregnancy) only doing it once in awhile—that is, not being promiscuous—is a form of protection. Whenever there is a message about the risks of promiscuity, educators need to clarify what creates the risks and why monogamy in itself does not provide safety.

Although the male-victim variant seems to have emerged first, there seem to be equal numbers of stories circulating with men and women as the transmitters. This is interesting because the chances that an infected man can pass HIV infection to a woman through unprotected intercourse are at least 17 times that of the reverse situation (Padian, Shiboski, and Jewell, 1991). One "Welcome to the wonderful world of AIDS" story is about a young man whose friends buy him a prostitute as a birthday present:

> It was this guy's eighteenth birthday, so his friends got together and chipped in and got him a hooker. When they were left alone in a hotel room, he told her he didn't really want to do it, he had just gone along so he wouldn't look like a wuss in front of his friends. She told him that she'd already been paid one way or the other, so why didn't he just relax and enjoy his present. She finally managed to convince him. After it was over he got up and took a shower. When he came back into the room, she was gone and written on the mirror in red lipstick were the words, "Welcome to the wonderful world of AIDS."

This story reinforces the belief about female prostitutes as reservoirs of infection, when, in fact, prostitutes are more at risk from their customers than the reverse and generally would require condoms if they could. Whatever the odds, it is important for both women and men to know there is a risk of contracting HIV whenever there is unprotected sex.

Another important accurate point these stories convey is that it is impossible to tell who is HIV positive. The infecting partners in these stories are young, attractive, charming, nice, well dressed. This is a welcome change from the reasoning of high school students who explain they do not have to worry about safe sex because they only go out with "nice" people or that they would be able to tell who is HIV positive. On the negative side, these stories are about sexual contact with "strangers," that is, someone they have met outside of the safe context of the home community, or sometimes a person who comes into the home community but does not belong. College versions of the "Welcome to the wonderful world of AIDS" stories involve people who meet on spring break in Florida or other specific vacation locations. College students report that this story is told frequently before spring break or summer vacation, and many say they were warned in high school before breaks by teachers, chaperons, and even police officers who told variants of this story. Other stories may involve business trips and conventions. Recently, the events have been increasingly located on a trip overseas. Unfortunately, these support the view that the "stranger" is the one who is dangerous. Lorenzo in the earlier story is a "stranger" both by location and ethnicity, while another version has the same role played by a Jamaican man. In one version, the woman stays at home but the "stranger" comes into her safe space:

> This girl went to the University of Florida, and she was staying there over Thanksgiving break. Well, this guy had come there to stay with a friend, or so he said, and they ran into each other in the mall. The guy asked this girl out. Normally she wouldn't have gone out with a stranger, but she was so lonely because everyone else had gone off for break that she said yes. They went out to dinner and talked for hours. He told her all about how hard a time he had finding a girl he could really talk to. He also told her that he was sorry he had met her when he was only going to be in the country another week.

The story continues with the usual courtship, ending with the tiny coffin. One woman said she had first heard the "Welcome to the wonderful world of AIDS" tale when she was living in South Dakota. At that time, according to the informant, South Dakota was the last state without a reported case of AIDS. Under those circumstances, the danger clearly seemed to lurk "out there." She said everyone felt safe in the state, but the story circulated at bars and was about a pick-up at a bar out of state. In Newfoundland, where the woman's story tends to take place during the family's winter retreat to Florida or another warm climate and the man's story tends to involve a one-night stand with somebody (often a prostitute) from the mainland, the legends provide a very strong lesson about "safe us" versus "dangerous other." In her article on this legend in Newfoundland, Goldstein (1992) emphasizes the importance in the legend of the risk as coming from outside: "In short, the message is that Newfoundlanders who stay home, don't get involved with Mainlanders, and don't engage in the violation of cultural norms, are not seen as being 'at risk'—despite participation in risky behaviors" (p. 37). The Newfoundland legends teach that safe sex is sex with another Newfoundlander.

A recent study examined sexual risk behavior in young people traveling abroad from the United Kingdom (Bloor et al., 1998). The authors found that about 10 percent of young travelers in the study reported sexual intercourse with a new partner, with 75 percent of this group using condoms on all occasions. Those who were on holiday were more likely to report a new relationship. There were some interesting gender differences, with a higher percentage of men reporting a new sexual relationship but with women more likely to report four or more sexual encounters. In addition, men's sexual risk behavior was consistent with behavior at home—that is, if they used condoms at home, they were likely to use them in these new sexual relationships. However, this consistency was not the case with women, whose sexual behavior while traveling was influenced by the characteristics of their new sexual partners, suggesting that the man has more of a say in the decisions about condom use. People who carried condoms with them were very likely to practice safer sex. It seems that, as some of the legends suggest, women may be more vulnerable to risky sexual encounters when traveling than when they are at home.

Students often say they are safe because they only become sexually involved with classmates from their own school, a variation on adolescents' beliefs in their own invulnerability. Not only they, but their entire schools, are protected just by being "self" and not "other." The "stranger danger" approach fell into disfavor in child abuse prevention education because it was recognized that the danger is more likely to come from someone the child knows and trusts—family, neighbors, babysitters. It is also necessary for sexuality/health educators to deal directly with the belief in "stranger danger" around HIV transmission, which serves to divert attention from risky behaviors to a vague risk group of "stranger." Students need to know that safer sex precautions are necessary no matter who the partner is. As mentioned above, Bolton (1992) discusses the dangers that can arise from messages about "knowing your partner" which help create "the perception that it [is] safe to have sex with people one [knows] because they couldn't possibly be infected" (p. 39, cited in Sobo, 1995, p. 30).

One indication that students are beginning to recognize the possibility of AIDS in their own group comes in a legend prevalent in an Athens, Georgia, high school in the spring of 1996, which claimed that 35 percent of donors at a student blood drive tested positive for HIV. The legend received enough attention to be debunked on the front page of the local newspaper (Manzione, 1996). A Red Cross representative was quoted as saying that the rumor had been attached to various high schools around the Southeast since 1991. One side effect of the legend has been that blood donations drop due to students' misguided fear that they might get AIDS from *giving* blood. However, there is a positive effect of such rumors and legends, in so far as they serve as warnings that you cannot assume people are "safe" just because you know them or because they attend your school. For example, one student reported:

One legend I heard growing up was there's "someone" at school who went to give blood when the Red Cross visited and the county health department informed the school that AIDS was found in contaminated blood. The rumor went around every year unfounded and not proven. But it did serve as a reminder that anyone you know could be infected.

Stories about an unidentified individual at *your* school being HIV positive are good antidotes to the belief that people you know can't be infected.

HIV as a Weapon

A last point is that these stories project a fear that people with HIV infections are out for revenge by infecting anyone they can. Part of this may be based on the reports of Patient Zero, who, according to stories, knowingly infected other men (Shilts, 1987). The belief is so strong that when a woman, as a hoax, called into a radio station claiming that she was HIV positive and was sexually active with men, there was no hesitation in accepting the story. (The young woman, when she was traced, said she did this as a warning to people to be careful.) Goldstein (1992) refers to such a story in Newfoundland:

> In the past year a story has circulated in St. John's, which one of my student assistants called the "Top Forty." In this story a St. John's resident who is HIV positive is determined to infect forty people who are on a list. He frequents local bars in order to pick up women and infect them, but, according to the story, everyone knows who he is and as a result no one will accompany him home, thereby thwarting his mission. (P. 26)

This of course combines the HIV positive person as vengefully infecting others with the theme of the safety of home. This fear of deliberate infection can be placed in the broader context of the fear of sudden, anonymous violence; these stories are essentially sexual drive-by shootings. Events reported in the news reinforce the messages of the legendry. In 1998, a man from East St. Louis, Illinois, who was HIV positive and had apparently deliberately had unprotected sex with over 100 women, infecting at least thirty, was found murdered. This followed the news reports of a man in Mayville, New York, who had infected at least nine women. In Tennessee, a woman, widowed and divorced, sought revenge against a former boyfriend who had infected her with HIV by having a series of one-night stands with men she met in bars (Associated Press, 1998). These news stories about "AIDS Marys," as they have been referred to, got national attention because they tapped right into shared fears. The latter one also enacts the male-victim version of the "Welcome to the wonderful world of AIDS"; the woman claimed she told her lovers that she was HIV positive, but we assume that this revelation occurred after the sexual contact.

There are also a number of stories about HIV being used as a weapon in nonsexual situations. For example, there are a number of legends/stories of someone walking on the street who is suddenly stuck with a syringe that is HIV infected or about moviegoers in a darkened cinema being stabbed from behind with infected needles. Another story is about a convenience store robbery in which the thief uses a syringe loaded with blood, which he claims is HIV infected, as his weapon. As with a gun aimed at you, it is unlikely you will take the risk of acting as if it were not loaded. In some self-defense classes, claiming to have AIDS is suggested as a way of preventing rape. One legend begins with a woman using that tactic and ends when the rapist says, "That's ok. So do I." A warning circulated extensively by e-mail in 1999:

> For your information, a couple of weeks ago, in a Dallas movie theater, a person sat on something sharp in one of the seats. When she stood up to see what it was, a needle was poking through the seat with an attached note saying, "you have been infected with HIV." The Centers for Disease Control in Atlanta reports similar events have taken place in other cities recently. All of the needles HAVE tested positive for HIV. The CDC also reports that needles have been found in the coin return areas of pay phones and soda machines.

The warning continues, explaining that this information originated in the Dallas police department and that the message comes from a sergeant who is the "USAF Safety Rep." Both of these pieces of information, along with invoking the name of the Centers for Disease Control, validate this as a "real" story (which it is not). Besides appearing in e-mail warnings, these stories circulate, as legends usually do, in casual conversation:

Today a friend of mine told me this story about this gang in Atlanta who puts needles with HIV in the coin returns of pay
phones so that when people go to get their change they get
stuck and become infected with HIV. This sounded like a legend to me, although I guess it could be true.

After my friend told me about the gang in Atlanta, I told my
roommates, and one of them told me about a legend she had
heard from a friend in which a girl was at the movie theater and
felt a pin prick in the back of her shoulder. She didn't really
think anything of it, but when she was walking out her friend
saw a sticker on her back which said "Welcome to the wonderful world of AIDS."

Unlike the stories in which there is a person who actively stabs someone, those of needles planted in seats or coin returns present a sense of
more pervasive danger always lurking—when you sit down, when you
retrieve your change, etc. In 1999, these stories had become the predominant legend about HIV infection. Their power is seen in the example of the student who reported that her mother called before a trip
specifically to warn her to take a cell phone so she would not need to use
a pay phone.

Trying to place those fears in perspective, rather than focusing on one
group (HIV positive people) as the enemy or on rare random events, can
be an important exercise. Sobo (1995) reports that most participants in
her condom use study related second-hand stories about deliberate or
accidental transmission of HIV which were then used to argue against
condom use, saying we can get infected no matter what we do, so why
bother with condoms? It is essential for people to know that, although
there is always a chance of unpredictable risks, there are ways to reduce
the predictable ones. Even if there is a minuscule risk that a random act
of violence will harm you, there is no reason to give up on everything
else that may make life safer. Sometimes analogies from other areas help
to get this point across. For example, occasionally, planes do fall out of

the sky and hit cars, but this doesn't mean we should all give up the life-saving practice of wearing seatbelts.

Other Dangers of AIDS Folklore

It is possible that the "AIDS Mary" from Tennessee had heard "Welcome to the wonderful world of AIDS" legends before embarking on her series of one-night stands. Health educators should be alert to other folklore about AIDS from which people may learn dangerous practices. In a process called ostension, people sometimes enact a legend which, until that time, had no basis in fact but only in people's fears. Such was the case with the long-circulating stories about razor blades and poison in Halloween candy. Parents and hospitals busily checked and x-rayed candy for years before the first actual case, which apparently happened when a father poisoned his son's Halloween candy and used the legendry as cover for the murder (Grider, 1984). As mentioned earlier, we piece together much of our information about sexual practice from folklore sources, and just as popular media may inspire certain dangerous behavior, so can folklore.

Health educators should be aware of dangerous beliefs as they begin to spread, such as the belief that AIDS can be cured through intercourse with a virgin. Legends about HIV positive men who rape young girls in order to cure themselves are currently told in parts of Africa and India but, given the speed with which folklore travels, especially in the age of electronic communication, these legends will probably appear in the United States very soon (if they have not already). The belief has precedence in the nineteenth- and early twentieth-century English and American belief that a man with venereal disease could cure himself by intercourse with a virgin (Hall, 1991) and in the more specific belief reported recently in the United States that "syphilis can be gotten rid of by 'giving it to a virgin'" (O'Connor, 1991). The belief goes back at least to the nineteenth century; in

1884 a man in England was tried for raping a fourteen year old in hope of curing his syphilis (Hall, 1991). Hall notes that this belief persisted into the twentieth century:

> This superstition was still prevalent thirty years later, being mentioned in evidence to the Royal Commission of Venereal Diseases in 1913:
>
> > A certain superstition exists that if a man has contracted venereal disease and he can have connexion with a virgin he will transmit that disease to her and escape himself free; the idea has existed for a very long time, I'm afraid. (P. 44)

In the 1990s the belief was connected to rape trials of HIV positive men in Zimbabwe and South Africa (Goldstuck, 1994). At a women's health conference in 1996, an international health expert mentioned in her speech that there were numerous reports of men who had acted on this belief about how to cure AIDS. More recently, it was reported in *Newsweek*, certainly a mainstream publication, that in some places in Africa "a widespread belief is that sex with a virgin, including girls as young as 10, can cure AIDS" (Will, 2000, p. 64). The cure does not always depend on a virgin. For example, in the United States in the 1940s, Randolph reported, "When backwoods boys acquire a dose of gonorrhea, they believe it can be cured by infecting as many females as possible" (1992, p. 880). When we first discussed in a paper these beliefs about curing disease (Henken and Whatley, 1995), a health and sexuality educator wrote a letter to us in which she said that her teenage clients often believe that when someone says, "you can give someone gonorrhea," it means you not only give it to someone, but also that you give it *away*, that is, get rid of it yourself. In terms of disease transmission, this makes no sense, but in terms of how language is used, it does. To give someone something usually means giving it away completely; it would be easy to interpret giving someone a disease in the same way. The tiny gift-wrapped coffin in the story then serves as a symbolic version of *giving* someone AIDS. AIDS educators need to clarify their terminology so that it is clear that giving does not mean giving *away*.

A number of legends and rumors circulating about AIDS can serve to undermine any success health education has had in terms of safer sex. For example, a story that was reported by Africa Online, Inc. in 1996 refers to a researcher who claims that condoms sent to Africa, as well as other developing countries, have been infected with the AIDS virus. The researcher claims to have taken samples and found them all "laced with the virus." An expert on AIDS in Africa confirmed in a personal conversation that this story had circulated and that she believed it had set back educational efforts to increase condom use as a method of AIDS prevention by several years.

Schoepf (1995) reports that in 1986 in Zaire, young urban men reinterpreted AIDS as an imaginary disease, rewriting SIDA, the French acronym for AIDS, as "Syndrome Imaginaire pour Decourager l'Amour" (Imaginary Syndrome to Discourage Love). He reported that the belief was that Europeans were using stories of an imaginary disease to discourage Africans from being lovers and that the motivation stemmed from jealousy. While Schoepf claims that those who used this reinterpreted acronym saw Europeans as motivated by jealousy, a similar view in some African American communities connect alleged misinformation about AIDS to attempts to keep African Americans from reproducing. The story is that AIDS is not actually caused by the HIV virus and is not transmitted by sexual intercourse. The public health education campaigns are seen as targeted at African American communities for the purpose of getting men to use condoms so that there will be fewer pregnancies. Condoms are seen as a useless form of prevention which serves a genocidal purpose, both by preventing reproduction and by not dealing with the "real" cause of AIDS.

Patricia Turner (1993) discusses a different set of rumors in African American communities which focus on AIDS as the result of experimental testing or intentional use of germ warfare targeted at specific groups. Some of these rumors say that the AIDS virus was specifically released in Africa, Haiti, or in U.S. African American communities, either to test out the virus as a weapon on a "disposable" population or as a deliberate genocidal plan. The spread of the disease to heterosexual white populations in the United States is believed to be a mistake resulting from the plan getting out of control. When placed in a context of a history of medical experimentation on African Americans and of racism in the health care system, this belief is understandable. One of the most infamous examples is the Tuskegee Syphilis Study, in which a number of African American men who had syphilis were studied to follow the natural course of the disease, without being given any information about it nor any treatment even after antibiotics became available. However, Vanessa Gamble (1997) presents a clear and compelling historical argument to explain attitudes in African American communities toward the biomedical system, pointing out that mistrust cannot be solely attributed to the Tuskegee Syphilis Study. Her article also traces the links to the current rumors about AIDS as a genocidal plot and concludes:

> Beliefs about the connection between AIDS and the purposeful destruction of African Americans should not be cavalierly dismissed as bizarre and paranoid. They are held by a significant number of Black people. For example, a 1990 survey conducted by the Southern Christian Leadership Conference found that 35% of the 1056 Black church members who responded believed that AIDS was a form of genocide. (P. 1775)

In analyzing this folklore, the significance is not whether the genocidal plot is true or even scientifically plausible, but the fact that so many people believe it to be true. The extent of acceptance of this rumor indicates the deep mistrust many African Americans have of the health care and scientific communities.

One folklore student collected folklore about the origins of AIDS

83

from a group of medical specialists (all men in their twenties) in the army reserve. The one African American man in the group said AIDS had been developed as a biological weapon in the United States for use against the Russians but when the Cold War ended, the government decided to use it against African Americans and other minorities, because:

> We're [African Americans] gaining too much power and numbers and they're afraid we're going to take over one day so they throw this shit at us, and it worked kinda, except that it's infecting everyone now, not just us. It backfired in their fucking faces, huh? Now it's gonna kill us all. Serves 'em right. I also heard there's a cure. I mean they wouldn't release something like this without a cure, right? Well those that sent, that set it loose, they're immune—people like the president, too, they're immune, real important, who you know aren't going to die, they get it, they get the cure. I guess that's who you gotta be these days to be safe.

It is an interesting variation in that the biological warfare is alleged to have been developed originally for the enemy outside and, with the loss of that enemy, the warfare was directed internally. The purported existence of both a cure and a means to become immune heightens the distrust of the government, which could release the cure but does not.

Not surprisingly, the other men participating in this discussion did not focus on AIDS as a racist genocidal plot. One man attributed it to God, rather than the government:

> God, because He's upset with all the evil things going on here in the world, has decided to wipe out all of humanity and teach us a lesson for being so bad . . . kind of like the Flood or the Black Plague. Um, so He sent AIDS, something that He knew we wouldn't be able to cure.

Another man, married and white, agreed that it was sent by God, though specifically aimed at gay men:

Anyways, God was being pissed off about there being so many fags and decided to do something about it, so He sends AIDS. And that's why they were the first to be infected. And that's how God intended it . . . Well, AIDS has taken care of that. It will start to dwindle off as the fags die off, them and the drug users, but that's why it's here, because God's trying to get rid of those gays.

This kind of rhetoric about God's punishment of gay men, prevalent at the beginning of the epidemic when focus was on gay men and intravenous (IV) drug users, led to the category of so-called "innocent victims," those who were born with HIV, or got it from blood transfusions or other blood products. The designation of this category has been strongly critiqued on the basis that no one "deserves" AIDS. The last speaker seems in denial about the fact that heterosexual men and women who do not use IV drugs also become HIV positive.

These kinds of rumors or beliefs about origins are not confined to informal discussions among friends, but become part of public discourse. For example, the African American actor Will Smith was quoted in a Sunday newspaper column: "I absolutely believe that AIDS is a result of testing in biological warfare. I think it was introduced into the homosexual communities in America" (Associated Press, 1997, p. 7A). While the article was written in a somewhat humorous tone, when a public figure cites these theories, the theories may gain credibility. It is interesting that Smith's statement focuses on the gay community as the target, rather than on African Americans. One international version of these biological warfare legends appeared in an Egyptian newspaper; an article reported that Israel used the AIDS and hepatitis viruses to contaminate blood supplies sent to Arab and Third World nations (*Response,* 1999).

The folklore about HIV as part of a biological warfare campaign functions in the same way as the folklore about the HIV virus as a weapon of random violence, serving to counter messages about the benefits of any behaviors, such as condom use, that reduce risk. Sobo (1995) writes:

Those who believe this argue that, because they are targeted to die, Black "AIDS victims" cannot be blamed for their sickness. Some also say that HIV infection is unavoidable, because the White Establishment will find a way around self-protective acts, perhaps by putting HIV in prelubricated condoms or using HIV test needles to inject the virus directly into the blood of the target-group members. This theory casts Black "AIDS victims" as innocent and helpless. Further, since population growth is a way of insuring that a people will not be silenced or die out, some Blacks who see AIDS as part of a deliberate attempt at genocide will advocate condomless sex because it permits conception. Unsafe sex becomes an act of resistance to oppression. (P. 39)

If it is believed that a cure exists (even if only the president and friends have it right now), there may be less fear of the disease and less protection. However, the overall effect would more likely be a sense of helplessness, that is, there is nothing that can be done to prevent becoming HIV positive. If "they" want to "get" someone or some group, "they" will. In an interesting twist, one student reported having heard from his father that:

The Russians developed the AIDS in a laboratory and are using it against us in germ warfare. . . . Our government has a cure for the AIDS but they won't release it. They're using it for population control.

Even though, according to this story, AIDS was developed to be used against the United States, the U.S. government has capitalized on the disease for population control. Meanwhile, it is assumed that only certain people will be allowed to benefit from the cure. In any case, these conspiracy theories make individual decisions and choices meaningless, except perhaps as individual acts of resistance.

Religious theories about the origin of AIDS also serve to undermine HIV/AIDS prevention. After all, if AIDS is God's punishment for homosexuality, then heterosexual believers are protected by God and have no need to take precautions. If a group thinks God is using disease to punish certain other groups, then following the right religion and not sinning (by the definitions of that religion) will save them. These theories may serve to reduce anxiety and fear in certain groups, but certainly would do nothing to help prevent transmission of HIV. To those who believe religious theories about AIDS, both the conspiracy theories and scientific theories are equally implausible/wrong. Those who do not believe the religious theories can turn to conspiracy theories or, perhaps, to a more "scientific" view of the disease process. If, for example, they believe that the HIV virus arose spontaneously and naturally, and that others, like the Ebola virus, could at any time develop and spread, then they may recognize that no one is ever "safe" simply by virtue of religious beliefs or membership in certain groups. The only hope would be in trying to learn what might prevent spread of the disease and behaving in ways that might reduce risk.

Beliefs about AIDS

The same approach that we suggested for discussing beliefs about pregnancy can be used in AIDS education. Asking students to collect beliefs from peers, family, and community members about how HIV is transmitted or how its transmission can be prevented provides a very useful starting point for teaching about transmission issues. Because students do not need to state whether they actually believe anything they contribute, this approach prevents possible embarrassment. Some beliefs may be derived from a class discussion of AIDS legends, such as:

You can't get HIV if you are monogamous.
You can tell who is HIV positive.
You are most at risk for HIV/AIDS from strangers.

Some of the common false beliefs, repeatedly debunked in AIDS education literature, are used in research that charts changes in knowledge about HIV/AIDS. These misconceptions include:

You can get AIDS from mosquitos.

You can get AIDS from toilet seats.

You can get AIDS from food prepared or served by someone who is HIV positive.

When a list of such statements to identify as True/False or Agree/Disagree are provided as part of a research instrument to investigate knowledge levels of a group, the research may be missing some very important misunderstandings. There are many false beliefs that researchers and educators fail to deal with simply because they don't know people hold these beliefs. One group working on AIDS issues with Asian women in Massachusetts (Collective Members, 1998, p. 32) found some dangerous misconceptions:

Only anal sex transmits HIV.

Nothing can be done to prevent a baby from getting AIDS during pregnancy/delivery.

A shower after sex reduces the risk of getting AIDS.

Withdrawal by a man before orgasm prevents transmission of HIV.

The belief about anal sex is an obvious offshoot of AIDS information that focused on gay men as a "risk group," with the implication that it is specific sexual practices that create the risk. This approach ignored the facts that many heterosexuals practice anal sex and that other sexual practices such as vaginal sex are very risky. While it is absolutely essential that men who have sex with men continue to get good AIDS education, sometimes the emphasis on gay men can have unintended consequences. On one end of the spectrum is the belief that only anal sex can transmit the virus, while on the other end is the belief that heterosexuals don't need to worry about anal sex because it is only gay men who get AIDS that way. One AIDS educator, Amber Hollibaugh, reported several years ago that a number of cases of HIV infection among teenage Latinas in New York were related to unprotected anal sex, practiced in order to preserve their virginity and keep boyfriends. These young women never considered anal sex a risk because all the education about anal sex was targeted to gay men.

Regarding the second belief above, there is now good scientific evidence that treating HIV positive pregnant women with the drug ZDV, formerly and still commonly known as AZT, can greatly reduce the risk of transmission of HIV to the fetus. The belief about the benefits of a shower is similar to some of the beliefs about the role of water in reducing risk of pregnancy; it needs to be explained very clearly that external washing will *not* remove the virus if it is inside the vagina, though there are benefits from washing in removing the virus from other parts of the body. Careful hand washing is a key step in taking universal precautions; the virus is fragile and won't survive on the skin for long, especially with good washing. The last belief also relates to beliefs about pregnancy prevention, but withdrawal is even less effective in preventing HIV transmission than in preventing pregnancy. If there are any sores, cuts, or abrasions on the penis, transmission can occur from these without ejaculation and, in addition, there may be preejaculatory release of seminal fluid, ranging from a drop to almost a flow, which could contain the virus. It is true that without ejaculation, there will be a lower viral load transmitted, but a lower load does not mean there is no risk. Relying on coitus interruptus is a very risky approach to AIDS prevention. Unless someone actually collects these beliefs, as the AIDS prevention group did in Massachusetts, educators will not know which misconceptions to address and they may discuss toilet seats and mosquitos when they should be talking about showers and withdrawal.

Some of the beliefs that can lead to dangerous practices are unintended offshoots of AIDS education, as several examples throughout this chapter illustrate. When giving accurate scientific information,

89

educators don't always think of the implications. For example, it is common to mention that a 1:10 dilution of bleach will kill the HIV virus. The educator often assumes the learners will know that the bleach is used to clean surfaces on which bodily fluid has spilled or to clean syringes or other equipment. The educator is probably not thinking that a woman who has had unprotected vaginal intercourse might decide to use bleach to douche herself after learning that bleach can kill the virus. The bleach itself can be harmful to the woman and probably won't reduce risk. Constantly monitoring potential misunderstandings or misuses of our teaching, while keeping current on beliefs and legends in the communities we serve, will help ensure that we are providing the most appropriate and useful education we can. In the area of HIV/AIDS, the risks of lack of good education can be deadly.

6

OF GERBILS AND STOMACH PUMPS

Homophobia in Legends

❑

A few years ago, apparently in Los Angeles, Richard Gere had to go to, into a hospital to have a gerbil removed from his posterior. . . . The doctor on call at the emergency room called in some, well this time he called it into a news station or radio station and it was passed around that way. But Richard Gere denied that one. But apparently—my brother lived out in Los Angeles when this supposedly took place and he said they were talking about it on the radio like it was fact. So Richard Gere denied it but I guess the jury's still out on that one.

In an episode of *ER*, the very popular television show about a Chicago emergency room, when an X-ray shows a large flashlight located inside a man's rectum, the staff jokes about his explanation that he accidentally sat on it while he was changing a fuse. Ask any emergency room staff and they will have stories about strange objects found in men's rectums, along with the patients' bizarre explanations of how those objects got there, always with the insinuation that the men are gay. One joke draws on this hospital lore:

Q: How many perverts does it take to screw in a light bulb?
A: One, but it takes a whole emergency room to get it out.

But not all the objects are inanimate and not all the men are nameless, since many of the stories are about gerbils and Richard Gere. The story is so well known that in Australia when the question was posed as to whether anyone knew any stories about gerbils, the first responses named Richard Gere. If a famous person is rumored to be gay, legends such as these serve as confirmation, even if a listener is aware that they may be untrue, as was the informant who said "the jury's still out."

As with many forms of jokes, legends, and other folklore about gay men, the emphasis is much less on where a gay man may insert his penis than on what may be inserted into him. This focus emphasizes the difference in meanings ascribed to the role of the receptive compared to that of the insertive partner. In some cultures (including many prisons), a man who is the insertive partner in anal or oral sex with a man is not viewed as homosexual at all, from which it follows logically that the receptive partner is not really a man, even if, as in a prison situation, he performs the role unwillingly. One of the hundreds of variants on light bulb jokes is:

Q: How many men does it take to screw in a light bulb?
A: Only one. A man will screw anything.

In jokes, stories, and legends, the term "man" usually means heterosexual because gay men are specifically identified as homosexual. But apparently, the corresponding line to "A [heterosexual] man will screw anything" is that "a gay man will be screwed *by* anything." It has been pointed out that heterosexual men have a great fear of penetration of the anus, of "getting screwed" or of being treated as a woman. However, when the gerbil stories are reported, it is usually by men who identify as heterosexual. And these men discuss the stories in great detail. One woman reported that the Richard Gere story was told to her by someone who knew someone who was working at the hospital "when Richard

Gere came in and had to have a gerbil, or something, removed from his ass because he . . . I don't even know what the purpose is but he had gotten this gerbil up there and had to get it removed." In contrast, most of the stories collected from men indicate no doubts in their minds as to why and how the gerbil got there.

Not only are heterosexual men telling these stories mistakenly confident that gerbil-insertion is a common practice among gay men, but they also believe they can provide detailed instructions. For example, one explained that gay men shave the gerbils and put cocaine on their skins before inserting them. The assumption is that the cocaine can be absorbed through the rectal mucosa, giving the men a rush; it is not clear whether the cocaine also has an effect on the gerbil, but the shaving may be for the purpose of easy absorption through the gerbil's skin (which is unlikely in reality to have any effect) so that the gerbil also is stimulated. Another explained that the gerbil is first placed in the freezer so that the inactive gerbil is more easily inserted; it will then warm up and become active. Some explained that the gerbil is declawed first, the thought of claws being particularly disturbing to many listeners. Others gave details on how it is inserted, using cardboard tubes and other devices. One man described, using his hands in imitation of gerbil feet, the digging action of the gerbil which is allegedly what is so stimulating. It seems that heterosexual men are very involved in the details of a practice (real or imagined) of gay men and have carefully thought through how this might work. The gerbil legend is so common that there are jokes that depend on knowledge of it. For example:

Q: What did the brown gerbil say to the white gerbil in Los Angeles?

A: Hi, you must be new in town.

There are also rumors that certain pet stores have been closed down because they were selling large numbers of gerbils to be used for sexual purposes and this was considered cruelty to animals. One informant had heard these rumors in England. Interestingly, gerbil stories do not appear in folklore told by gay men; there is no mention of such stories by Goodwin (1989a) in his book on gay men's folklore and the author, as well as gay men interviewed about this, reported more recently that they are unaware of gerbils in either the practice or folklore of gay men. A book discussing emergency room procedures in the context of the show *ER* presented the hospital gerbil-extraction story as a "true account" (Gibbs and Ross, 1996). Even though this is presented as true, it would be interesting to know if this actually appears in any hospital's records or is merely a medical legend presented as true, since other researchers attempting to track it down have found no corroboration. One website (http://www.snopes.com/), which specializes in analyzing whether legends are true or not, claims there has never been a verified case of a rodent extracted from a patient's rectum. These stories are most likely heterosexual men's creations which serve the purpose of allowing them to discuss the taboo subject of anal penetration while distancing themselves in disgust.

The "ew, gross" reaction that this legend receives along with the insistence on its truth or at least feasibility (demonstrated by all the explanations of how exactly the gerbil is prepared, inserted, and enjoyed) has several dangerous aspects to it. It reinforces in the heterosexual community the idea that "they," that is, gay men, engage in unnatural acts and are capable of any bizarre or barbaric behavior that involves anal penetration. A second concern is that the ready acceptance of "gerbiling" as an actual practice of gay men might lead a naive young man, first discovering his homosexuality and lacking any reliable guidance, to attempt it. A third problem is the harm it does to the men whose names are associated with the legend. The legend was first attached to Richard Gere at a time (1990) when a resurgence of his career brought him into sudden prominence, and analyses suggest that the legend was used as a means to hurt his popularity (Dresser, 1994). The legend had previously been attached to a popular Philadelphia television personality who, although not fired (as claimed in subsequent versions of the legend), did have his career adversely affected (Vorpagel, 1988). Along with a student from Philadelphia reporting the legend from his home town, students from Augusta reported that the story had been spread about their local top-rated news anchor, who was then fired. Whether or not these men were actually fired, one can see the danger that it could happen.

In Dresser's (1994) paper on "gerbiling," she discusses how these kinds of legends can fuel homophobic behavior. She describes a terrible incident at the University of Iowa in 1991, when a right-wing campus newspaper:

> produced a report on gerbiling which was presented as fact. They also displayed a large-sized parody of the AIDS quilt in the showcases near the campus Union Station dining area, using detailed images and pet names of so-called deceased gerbils, e.g., Cuddles, Varmint, Petey, Wilbur, and their ages at death. This took place during Freshman Orientation Week when many parents were on campus. (P. 239)

This and other related incidents drew on a legendary and completely undocumented behavior to attack gay men, including drawing in, according to Dresser, a gullible television reporter who reported gerbiling as fact.

Protecting Their Backsides

Heterosexual men's fear of penetration is very clearly presented in another legend:

> A student went to the doctor complaining of pain in his anus. The doctor claimed it was from anal intercourse, and the guy freaked out. He was not a homosexual and had never had anal intercourse, but the doctor said there was definitely evidence of this occurrence. Apparently his roommate was putting ether on his bed at night to knock him out and then proceeded to have

anal intercourse with him. He had seen the ether and Vaseline in the room, but this was not unusual, because the roommate was an entomology major. In the end, this roommate was kicked out of school.

This story was reported by a woman college student as told to her by her boyfriend. The style and language can be contrasted with a version told by one man college student to another about an event in a dormitory on campus:

> This guy, hm, this guy. This guy's roommate. This guy's butt was bleeding. His ass was bleeding when he went to the bathroom. So he went to the infirmary up at Gilbert Health Center, and was like, "I really got a problem. I don't know what's going on or what. My ass really hurts when I take shits and stuff." The doctor was like, "Well to tell you the truth you need to stop your homosexuality for awhile." The guy was like, "Wait a minute. I'm not queer. I have never had sex in the ass by another man." The doctor was like, "Well, [that's] what's been happening." And the guy was like, "I don't know how this could be; that's impossible." So a week goes on and he's still having this problem. And he goes back and the doctor said the same thing, "You have got to quit doing this." Come to find out his roommate was a flaming fag and had been getting ether and when they had gone to bed at night and was knocking him out and plugging him in the butt while he was asleep.

The language in this version expresses much more clearly the anxiety on the part of the teller—a man—than did the version told by a woman. The story itself is virulently homophobic, in its expression of the belief that gay men, especially "flaming fags," would go so far as to drug their roommates with ether in order to have anal intercourse with them. This also reverses the view of gay men as the receptive partner only. Contradictory images of gay men appear: the passive receptive partner—who is therefore not really a man—who will willingly be penetrated by any-thing, as opposed to the testosterone-driven sex maniac who is after every man's ass.

The gerbil story is one that distances heterosexual men from what are purported to be the practices of gay men, while the roommate story does not allow any safety through distance. It is instead used as a warning of the imagined dangers if gay men are allowed to live with heterosexual men. What more effective anti-gay legend could circulate at the time of intense debates about gays in the military? All the joking warnings not to bend over to pick up the soap in the shower assert that men can pro-tect themselves from penetration if they are alert to danger, but the roommate stories give the warning that you can *never* let your guard down, even in the apparent safety of your own bedroom. Many of the men in folklore classes had heard this story, most in senior year of high school or freshman year of college. Others had heard the same story after enlisting in the military, which makes it clear that any discussion of gays in the military is in the context of fears already expressed in leg-end. One student reporting this story concluded:

Apparently as he was sleeping the roommate was getting him. He beat the guy up bad. He didn't get convicted.

I heard this one before going off to school. I guess it was a way to scare me or something because I was going to stay in a dorm. Even though I figured that it wasn't a true story, I always kept an eye on my roommate.

A "safe sex" variant on the roommate legend recently appeared:

This guy has a rash in the rectal area and goes to the doctor. The doctor says, "This is easy to cure. The rash is from the condoms you're using; just change condoms." The guy says, "No, it can't be; I'm not gay." So he goes away, and the rash gets worse and he goes back to the doctor, who says, "I told you, just change your brand of condom." And the guy still says, "I'm not gay."

Then he's back in his room, and looking in his roommate's drawers for something, and this box of condoms rolls out.

When this variant was first reported in a class in 1995, most men in the class recognized the story but not the condom variant. A woman student reported hearing it her freshman year from a male friend who had just heard it. It is interesting that the presence of condoms in a man's room is considered proof that he is gay. For previous generations, condoms were "proof" that a man was heterosexually active, but the connection of gay men to AIDS to condoms for safer sex changes the meanings of condom-possession. This version did not even mention ether, though other versions now include condoms and ether. For students who had already heard the legend in another form, the mention of condoms is enough explanation, but apparently the presence of condoms was also sufficient for those who had not previously heard the story.

Heterosexual men's fears of being penetrated and the assumption that this is likely to occur in certain settings have been expressed in many forms in popular culture, often humorously. For example, in the film *House Party,* the adolescent rapper hero is locked in jail with a number of very threatening inmates who draw straws to decide who will have him first. Expecting to be bailed out soon, he tries to delay the assault by launching into a rap explaining why they should leave him alone. The rap includes references to AIDS, Rock Hudson, Liberace, "homos," and protecting his "back door." In the film *My Cousin Vinny* (1992, Twentieth Century Fox), the humor in one scene depends on the misunderstanding by a young man in prison who believes that the lawyer Vinny is a tough inmate who is going to rape him and his cellmate. Everything Vinny says is an unintentional double entendre that leaves the young man quivering in terror:

VINNY: What's wrong with you?
STAN: I don't want to do this.

VINNY: I understand, but, you know, what are the alternatives?

STAN: My alternatives? To what? To you? I don't know—suicide? Death?

VINNY: Look, it's either me or them. You're getting fucked one way or the other. Hey, hey, hey. Lighten up. OK? Don't worry; I'm gonna help you out.

STAN: Gee, thanks.

VINNY: Excuse me, but I think a modicum of gratitude would not be out of line here.

STAN: You think I should be grateful?

VINNY: Yeah, I mean it's your ass, not mine. I think you should be grateful. I think you should be down on your fucking knees.

Both these scenes, as well as the roommate legend, depend on the shared fear and obsession heterosexual men have about other men who are out to "get their asses." In these cases, popular media and folklore reinforce each other's messages.

The mixture of fear and fascination about anal intercourse in the media is well described by Simpson (1994) in his discussion of media presentations of issues around gays in the military:

The increasing difficulty of trying to enforce or even depict a demarcation between homosexuality and heterosexuality became even more apparent when TV news programmes attempted to illustrate the "problem" of gays in the military by showing endless footage of GI's taking showers: the hetero male's terrible anxiety that his best pal may make a pass at his ass depicted in shots of acres of ripe, naked young male ass. The attempt to depict the heterosexual male world of buddiness and virility, innocent of the taint of queerness, collapsed into voyeurism of the queerest kind: a televised military Mr. Hot Buns contest. (P. 5)

Punishing Gay Men

One form of reassurance for heterosexual men is that something bad happens both to men who voluntarily are the receptive partners in anal intercourse and to those who force themselves on unwilling, especially unconscious, men. After all, Richard Gere (whose alleged emergency room visits have been reported all over the country) would have been humiliated by a trip to the hospital to have a gerbil removed and then by the widespread knowledge of this alleged "emergency surgery." In some legends, the outcome is even worse for some gerbil users. In one story, the partner, who had inserted the gerbil using a cardboard tube, lights a match hoping the light will attract the gerbil so it will retreat from the rectum. In an Internet version, the legend is presented as a news story falsely attributed to the *Los Angeles Times*:

> At a hushed press conference, a hospital spokesman described what happened next. "The match ignited a pocket of intestinal gas and flame shot out the tube, igniting Mr. Tomazewski's hair and severely burning his face. It also set fire to the gerbil's fur and whiskers which in turn ignited a larger pocket of gas further up the intestine, propelling the rodent out like a cannonball." Tomazewski suffered second degree burns and a broken nose from the impact of the gerbil, while Farnum suffered first and second degree burns to his anus and lower intestinal tract.

The attribution of stories to a specific publication or television show helps convince readers or listeners of their veracity. Here the journalistic attribution carries more weight than the word of a friend of a friend. There are a number of variations on this legend, some including the gerbil's name and different ways of inserting the gerbil (the use of PVC pipe rather than a cardboard tube, for example). These stories are presented as if they are very humorous, although it seems likely that listeners would recognize second degree burns to the anus and lower intestinal tract as extremely serious and painful. Both the humor and the lack of compassion result from this story being about gay men who are seen as getting exactly what they deserve. Stories about the alleged use of gerbils by gay men in the United States have also been reported in England. In a humorous book called *Now! That's What I Call Urban Myths* (Healey and Glanvill, 1996), the authors report:

> A well-known practice among gay men in Los Angeles—and some Hollywood actors, it's said—of slipping a hamster or a gerbil up their partner's back passages (this apparently provides a highly pleasurable stimulation while the rodent scurries about) took a violent twist once when two loving partners tried it. (P. 214)

It continues with the story of the exploding gases, although the result is less terrible with only a nose broken in two places as the consequence.

Many versions of the roommate story do not specify what happened to the assailant, although some mention that he was expelled from school and one has the victim, after he has figured it out, picking up his baseball bat and waiting for the roommate to get back. Gay bashing by young men who use a variety of weapons, including baseball bats, is fairly common, so this version may have more meaning than simple revenge on a rapist; some may view it as an appropriate response to any gay man. In December, 1999, an 18-year-old private was found guilty of murdering a gay soldier by beating him to death with a baseball bat while he slept in his barracks. The gay soldier, after having been harassed for a long period of time, finally knocked down one of the main tormentors, who responded by killing him the next night (Clines, 1999). Homophobia, supported by such legends as the ones discussed in this chapter, helps fuel violent responses to gay men who have done nothing but try to go about their lives.

Another variant of the roommate legend focuses specifically on the punishment:

When I was at Tech there was a horrific story that went around. This story involved a freshman rooming with a chemical engineer who was an upperclassman. This freshman had an over-protective mother, who quite often would drop in unexpected. Mid-quarter the freshman began bleeding rectally with his early morning bowel movements. At the health center the doctor told him, "I believe you know exactly why your bleeding occurs." "No, I don't," replied the freshman. The doctor responded, "It's simple, stop having anal intercourse and the bleeding will end." One night, feigning sleep, the freshman caught his roommate with ether and a rag. Horrified, he called his mother, who came and consoled him. Later, the mother stalked and killed the roommate, throwing his body in the sewer. No evidence was ever found linking the mother to the engineer's violent death.

The storyteller states that the mother was overprotective but does not imply that the engineer's fate was inappropriate. Perhaps the message is that the freshman should have been a real man and taken it on himself to mete out punishment.

Fellatio and the Tell-Tale Sperm

While anal penetration is usually the focus of homophobic folklore, fellatio by men is a close second. Again it is the receptive partner who is portrayed negatively and again it is a chance to "confirm" suspicions about the sexual orientation of famous men:

Back in the 70s, when Rod Stewart, the rock musician, was on tour, apparently—I forget what city he was in, I think Amsterdam or something—as the story goes, he apparently had to go in the hospital to have his stomach pumped and apparently the

doctor on call said they found like half a quart of male semen in
his stomach and they had to pump it.

The man who relayed this story was the same one who reported the gerbil story at the opening of this chapter with a mix of skepticism and belief. The naming of famous rock stars serves to "confirm" rumors about
their homosexuality or bisexuality or to undermine a heterosexual
image that the star conveys; we heard the same story about David
Bowie, Elton John, Boy George, Bon Jovi, and, from New Kids on the
Block, the singer identified by the informant as the "most effeminate."
One informant explained that the reason she doubted the truth of the
story was that she had heard identical versions about Rod Stewart and
David Bowie. These stories are generally first heard about junior high
age (the star changing with the times) when students, faced with puberty and sorting out their own sexuality, are particularly intrigued by
the mixed messages of rock stars who play with images of androgyny,
bisexuality, and homosexuality. Some versions say only "some semen"
whereas others state specific amounts, up to two quarts. For those who
are wondering how many ejaculations it would take to provide that
much semen, an average ejaculation contains 3.5 milliliters (Denney
and Quadagno, 1988, p. 42), which means it would take about 286
ejaculations to equal one liter (a liter is 1.06 quarts). Even if the indus-
trious rock star could perform fellatio that many times, a lot of the
semen would probably have left his stomach before he completed the
job. A man who willingly swallows "male" semen (the inclusion of the
redundant "male" emphasizes the point that this is a homosexual act) is
considered as deviant as a man who allows a gerbil to be inserted anally.
A scene in the film *The Crying Game* illustrates this. When the central
character realizes that the "woman" who performed fellatio on him is actually a man, he runs to the toilet and vomits. Another film, *Ace Ventura, Pet Detective,* parodies this scene while at the same time reinforcing the intensity of disgust with male homosexuality. Ace Ventura,

realizing that he has kissed a man disguised as a woman, not only vomits into the toilet but also uses a toilet plunger on his mouth, brushes his teeth with an entire tube of toothpaste, burns all his clothes, and scrubs himself in the shower. This powerful disgust was reflected in a legend a male student collected from several other men:

> I heard a story about a guy and this girl on a date. The guy takes her to eat and then to a movie. After the movie, the guy and the girl go to the park. They leave after awhile and he drops the girl off at her dorm. When he gets back to the apartment he tells his friends about the date and how the girl did certain things. The next day, a guy comes to the house and tells the boy it was he that dressed up as a girl. The boy throws up and that's the end of the story.

In this version it is not clear what they actually did in the park, that is, how much he bragged to his roommates about activities that never happened. He could be vomiting because he realized he had been sexual with a man, behaving as the film characters did, or because his roommates now *believe* that he was sexual with a man.

There are many stories circulating about women and fellatio but these have a very different tone, since they are about heterosexual activity, as the three examples below illustrate:

> There is a legend told in Augusta about a girl who attended [one or the other of two specific high schools]. During a sex ed class the subject of semen entered the discussion. During the discussion the teacher provided the make-up of the fluid and stated that semen was high in glucose. Suddenly the girl raised her hand and blurted out, "Then why does it taste so salty?" Realizing what she had done, she ran out of the room and transferred to a different high school the next day.

> Last year (a friend of a friend) heard about a girl in her biology 103 lab doing an experiment where one scrapes the inside of

one's mouth and looks at the sample on a slide, with a micro-scope. Something odd was moving on the girl's slide so she called over two of the teaching assistants who looked at the sample and did not recognize what was on the slide. The group called in the professor who says, "Oh, that's a sperm."

This story I heard from a friend. . . . This supposedly happened at a college up north. It sounds a bit like a legend to me. A professor of biology was discussing the high glucose levels in semen when a young girl asked why semen didn't taste sweet if it was so high in glucose. After the words escaped her mouth, she was mortified and ran out of the classroom never to return. But the professor had a seemingly perfectly rational answer to her query. He said, "The taste buds for sweetness are on the tip of the tongue, not in the back of the throat."

One college student reacted to the question of how she and her high school friends responded when the sperm on the slide story had been told by a teacher in a high school Advanced Placement summer course:

It was like, some of the guys were like jeering at some of the girls, like "Girl, you shouldn't do it," or "You shouldn't do it." I mean just as jokes but, and so all the girls were sitting there getting the toothpicks [to do scrapings of cheek cells], going like, "I'll do it" cause you know, "I'm not afraid; nothing wrong with me; I don't have any sperm in my mouth." So I guess that's how they reacted.

The teasing by boys and the speed with which girls tried to prove they were not worried about being embarrassed illustrate the way this kind of story can be used to control young women's sexuality.

In the second story, we don't find out what happened to the young woman but it was obviously supposed to be extremely embarrassing; the consequences of a group finding out she was heterosexually active, having performed fellatio, may perhaps not be as damaging for a college student as one in high school. However, the location in the third story is college and the "young girl" never returned. Imagine, however, if a high school girl had to transfer because of the shame or a college woman student never returned, what would have happened if the story involved a high school *boy* or *man*. In these stories, the embarrassment is from accidentally revealing that a woman has been sexually active, but at least she is *heterosexually* active.

The celebrity stomach pump story has very recently appeared about a woman:

> My sister called me to tell me she had heard the singer Alanis Morissette passed out on stage and when they took her to the hospital, she had to have her stomach pumped because it was filled with tons of semen.

While this story labels a woman rock star as promiscuous, it also still labels her as heterosexual, so that it has a different impact than the stories about men. There is another female version (told by men!) of the stomach pump story. Fine (1992) reports this typical version he collected of the legend of "The Promiscuous Cheerleader":

> The story I remember from high school was of a University [of Minnesota] cheerleader who got her kicks by giving blow jobs to the basketball team, the players and that. And that she snuck down somehow, or I don't know if it was . . . I think it was before a game, or the night before a game or something. Uh, got it on with almost the entire team, gettin' off givin' 'em all suck jobs. And uh she got sick, during the game she fainted, and they had to take her away and she got a quart of cum in her. (P. 60)

Fine, commenting that the amounts range "up to four to six quarts," states:

> The mistaken amount of seminal fluid indicates exaggeration of the male's sexual prowess—perhaps serving a wish fulfillment

function. Further, since semen is largely protein, there is no medical rationale for pumping the girls' stomach. The stomach-pumping serves as a symbolic punishment. (P. 63)

While the stomach-pumping was certainly not necessary, the composition of semen is not primarily protein—it includes carbohydrates, proteins, salt, and sperm cells (Denney and Quadagno, 1988, p. 41), which is just as harmless a mixture.

Celebrity Gay Jokes

Often a news story creates an opportunity for jokes; shocking incidents, mass murders, and celebrity news stories all are considered fair game (See, for example, Goodwin, 1989b). For example, there have been many jokes about O. J. Simpson, John Wayne Bobbit, Jeffrey Dahmer, and Michael Jackson. Some of these jokes depend on both shared knowledge of the well-publicized events or people and a shared homophobia:

Q: How did the police find Bobbit's penis?
A: They hired a fag to sniff it out.

The celebrity golf tournament was a disaster: O. J. Simpson was slicing; Heidi Fleiss was hooking; Ted Kennedy drove into the water; Greg Louganis kept hitting the wrong hole.

Greg Louganis, an Olympic gold medalist in diving, had come out as gay, and the "wrong hole" is an obvious reference to anal intercourse. The Michael Jackson jokes draw on the shared knowledge about the accusations that he had been sexually involved with young boys:

McDonald's has a new item on their menu. It's called the Michael Jackson burger. It's got five inches of beef placed between two tiny little buns.

Q: What's the difference between Michael Jackson and acne?

A: Acne won't come on your face until you're thirteen.

Q: What did the Bishop say to Michael Jackson?

A: You molest one more young boy and I'll give you a Roman parish.

The first two Michael Jackson jokes draw on the allegations about the pop star's sexual activity with young boys and the assumptions about male homosexual activities. These jokes, like the legends, create an opportunity to discuss what otherwise cannot be discussed. Heterosexual men will not ordinarily chat with their friends about what gay men do, but these jokes provide the context to do that. The jokes and stories about celebrities are deliberately intended to diminish these famous people. The third joke draws on rumors and stories about Catholic priests involved sexually with boys; it gives the teller (and the listener) a chance to express both homophobia and anti-Catholic biases in the context of a joke. The rumors about Michael Jackson and the accompanying jokes also perpetuate the dangerous and incorrect belief that gay men sexually abuse boys. This belief has cast suspicion on gay men child care providers and school teachers, sometimes driving them from jobs or preventing their being hired, while ignoring the fact that the majority of child sexual abuse is committed by heterosexual men. This is not to imply that no gay man (nor any woman) could be guilty of child sexual abuse, but that this is unusual behavior on the part of gay men. Jokes like these keep the stereotypes fresh and powerful.

The folklore about gay men allows the opportunity for presumably heterosexual men to bring up subjects they would not ordinarily discuss, in the "safe" context of showing disgust toward the behavior of gay men. The detailed discussions of gerbiling indicate a fascination with a behavior that has not actually been documented as being practiced. The roommate legend provides warnings about the dangers that gay men allegedly pose but can also be seen as a warning about being in all-male environments—such as the military or fraternities. The celebrity jokes and legends serve to undermine the reputation of famous men; the rumor that a man is gay may not be very shocking now, so coupling it with a bizarre practice such as gerbiling or excessive fellatio makes the rumors more humiliating. Interestingly, homophobia focused on lesbians takes a different form, which will be discussed in the next chapter on women's sexuality.

What Educators Can Do

Discussing the folklore about gay men offers opportunities to confront misunderstandings and misinformation about gay men and challenge homophobic views. Homophobia is a powerful force in the lives of adolescents. For example, among high school students, one survey found that being called gay was considered more upsetting than being physically abused, with 17 percent of students reporting that this had happened to them (AAUW, 1993). Another survey found that of 3,210 high-achieving students, 29 percent admitted to anti-gay prejudice (*Advocate,* 1997). The Safe Schools Project in Washington State had 146 incidents of anti-gay harassment or violence reported to them over a five-year period (Safe Schools Coalition, 1999). According to the report, in addition to name-calling and other "milder" forms of harassment, violence directed at gay or lesbian students (or students thought to be gay) involved kicking, punching, using weapons, and gang rape. In one-third of the incidents, adults did nothing, but in one-third, at least one adult stood up for the child, sometimes with very positive results. Sometimes just the intervention by an adult to stop a student from gay-baiting or to explain why calling another student "faggot" is not acceptable was sufficient to end the harassing behavior. Silence by adults conveys the message that anti-gay behavior is acceptable. In a video about teaching gay and lesbian issues in the schools, *It's Elementary* (1996, Women's Educational Media), the principal of Cambridge

Friends School discusses the school's gay pride day and why they try to interrupt homophobia:

> When you allow a child on a playground to hurl an insult at another child or to say "your mom is queer" or to say those sorts of things without addressing the issues is, I think, unconscionable. What's the message the child gets? The child gets the message my teacher would step in if it was wrong. My teachers would do something.

In a study of lesbian step families, Janet Wright (1998) presented some examples of the kinds of incidents that make school harder for the children of lesbians:

> The children in this study did have a few overtly negative experiences with the schools. Talia, when she was in second grade, wanted to make two Mother's Day cards at school and her teacher said she could only make one. When Diana was a senior in high school, her moms sent one of her baby pictures in to the yearbook with the caption "From your two moms" and the picture was mysteriously lost and not printed. (P. 153)

The first example seems to be an example of a rigid approach, since there are many children, even those from heterosexual families, who might want to make a second Mother's Day card. The small ways in which these students' lives and families could have been validated would also help validate others who do not live in nuclear families. In addition, there would be a positive message for a student who is questioning or exploring his or her own sexuality. Even though educators in many communities find it challenging to figure out ways to introduce gay and lesbian positive messages or educational materials, it is essential, even in the most conservative communities, that educators plan positive ways to interrupt rampantly homophobic climates. The report from the Safe Schools Coalition gives many examples of successful intervention and also reports on some of the impact when nothing is done: twelve stu-

dents changed schools, ten dropped out of school, ten attempted suicide, two committed suicide.

In 1996, a Wisconsin school district agreed to pay a former student,
a gay man, $900,000 in an out-of-court settlement after a federal court
found the school administrators liable for not protecting the student
from anti-gay harassment and abuse. Since seventh grade he had en-
dured verbal harassment, a "mock rape," and physical assaults, including being knocked into a urinal and urinated on (*Educator's Guide to Controlling Sexual Harassment, 1997*). Timely intervention on the part of
teachers or administrators could have saved this student a great deal of
pain. After the terrible incident in Wyoming, in which a young gay
man, Matthew Shepard, was beaten and left to die, Congressman Bar-
ney Frank made an impassioned speech to the House of Representatives,
emphasizing the role schools could play:

> In particular, we have debated on the floor of this House meas-
> ures whereby Members have sought to penalize secondary
> schools for setting up programs to do two things. First, they
> would offer protection to the young gay men and lesbians who
> find themselves tormented and abused and sometimes physi-
> cally assaulted in school. Second, some of these schools would
> try to teach young people in their teens that brutalizing people
> because they don't like their sexual orientation is not acceptable
> human behavior.
>
> . . . These are people [the men who killed Matthew Shepard]
> not long out of high school themselves. This underlines the im-
> portance of allowing educators to deal with prejudice. (Frank,
> 1999, pp. 4–5)

Education in the schools needs to address homophobia directly, as it
should address racism, sexism, and other forms of discrimination. If
homophobic jokes surface in discussion, they should not be silently ignored. Confronting beliefs about gay men through examining contemporary folklore can help some students rethink their intense homophobia

that can result in harassment and violence. Examining why people are so willing to accept the roommate legend, for example, is an approach to undermining the false belief that gay men are predatory rapists. In this context, it is useful to discuss the fact that men who rape men most often identify as heterosexual. As mentioned earlier, gang-rape has been used against individuals who are assumed to be gay or lesbian. The discussion of why heterosexual men punish a gay man by sexually assaulting him exposes a strange contradiction. Clearly, the rapists don't see that by having anal intercourse with a man, they themselves are violating any norms, but instead see that as a way of punishing someone for the "crime" of loving another man. Folklore opens the possibility for some difficult but important explorations of the misunderstandings and biases that underlie homophobia.

Besides perpetuating homophobic stereotypes, some of this folklore can have other negative effects on young men or boys who are newly aware that they may be gay or bisexual. Coming out before the gay liberation movement meant there were few sources of information. Coming out stories involved searching secretively through libraries for references, usually finding negative ones that focused on psychopathology. Now there is a huge array of information and positive images in the popular media as well as gay presses. However, not all of this may be accessible and, even if there are positive images, that doesn't necessarily help a young man figure out what he needs to know about healthy sexuality and sexual behaviors. Hearing legends about gerbils and other things that men supposedly insert anally is not a helpful introduction to gay sexuality. Neither are the stories about gay men as predators. In the schools, it is already generally difficult to talk about heterosexual sexual behaviors, contraception, and safer sex, so it is not likely that discussions of safe anal intercourse and fellatio will be welcome. However, somewhere in community settings, if not in the schools, that information needs to be available. As well as benefiting gay men, it could also help heterosexual women, who certainly engage in fellatio and 30 percent of whom have reportedly had anal intercourse. Young women especially use anal intercourse as a means of contraception and/or a way of preserving their virginity until marriage, yet may be unaware of any of the health issues. A readily available source is *Our Bodies, Ourselves,* which, though it is a women's health book, has information men would also find useful. The basic information about anal intercourse or other anal stimulation includes such concepts as: that "the anus is not as elastic as the vagina" and therefore penetration should go slowly and a lubricant should be used; there are many bacteria and other infectious agents in the colon so care must be taken to avoid spreading infection (use of dental dams, condoms, gloves; if following anal penetration with vaginal penetration or oral sex, change condoms or wash thoroughly); the rectal membranes are delicate and easily torn so there is also more risk of blood-borne infections such as HIV, so the above precautions are even more essential (Boston Women's Health Book Collective, 1998, p. 245). For more details on other forms of anal stimulation and on other sexual activity between men, there are publications in very accessible forms from various organizations such as the Gay Men's Health Crisis. Health and sexuality educators should provide information that young gay and bisexual men need in order to engage safely and pleasurably in sexual activity. Folklore can provide an entry point for discussions that would otherwise never occur.

7

THE PEANUT BUTTER SURPRISE

Fear and Loathing of Women's Sexuality

❏

There is a girl and she is home with her parents. Well, she is up in her
bedroom and she has this hot dog she took from the refrigerator. She is
masturbating with the hot dog and it gets stuck. She is freaking out, and
she has to go to the hospital to get the hot dog out. So she goes downstairs
and tells her parents that she has to go to the hospital. They take her to
the hospital and the doctor comes in. She tells the doctor her predicament
and he does the surgery to remove the hot dog lodged up in her.

There is a clear message in this legend for young women who experi-
ment with sexuality; the result of attempts at masturbation for this
teenager is humiliation of the most dramatic kind, involving both her
parents and an emergency room visit. In her analysis of the legend,
which was popular in her middle school and high school, the student
who collected it commented on the girl's anxieties about sex leading her
to masturbate, "which is taboo anyway," and the embarrassment of talking about sex with her parents. She might have also discussed the fear
of objects not only getting stuck, but also disappearing, in the vagina,
which is a common fear, especially among young adolescents. Combin-

ing common anxieties about sexuality with lack of basic knowledge of anatomy, the stories have achieved wide circulation.

Stories about objects stuck in vaginas are counterparts of the stories of objects in the rectums of gay men, again linking the sexuality of gay men and women. There are many versions of what gets stuck in the vagina and what the consequences are, and it is clear from the comments included with the legends that they do give strong messages to girls in upper elementary and middle school:

> Several stories I heard growing up which made my vagina frightening to me. I remember one in particular which had several variations. A girl roughly my age (elementary school) stuck a hot dog/pickle/carrot into her vagina and part of it broke off. She was so embarrassed that she couldn't tell anyone. It rotted and killed her. (The other version ended with the shame she felt when she broke down and asked for help.)

> A legend I heard in sixth grade . . . At this time there was a girl that supposedly was wondering [what] penetration felt like, so she tried a hot dog. I was told it broke off in her, and they had to take her to the emergency room. Although I can't remember her name, it was a particular girl. . . . She had large breasts and was teased about being easy with the boys.

> There was a girl I went to junior high with who had a legend about her. She was an unusual girl who had several unusual behavior problems. She was not well accepted among everyone. It was told that she had masturbated with a hot dog and had to go to the emergency room to have it removed after part had broken off and gotten lost.

> When I was in California I'd heard this story about this girl who had gotten a frozen hot dog stuck up, up her vagina, and um, 'cause she was like masturbating or something, and it was frozen and she had to go to the hospital and get it surgically removed.

And it was this girl who had already graduated or whatever, and it was kind of like I mean when I lived in California you based it, I mean, they used to tell stories to the freshmen all the time. But then I moved to Maryland and I heard the same thing, but it wasn't a frozen hot dog, it was just a regular hot dog. And the same thing, except for this girl, it was someone who I knew of, I didn't know really anybody there, but I knew of the girl, and they were like, "ooh, that's her," that's the girl, you know who it happened to. She was so shy she probably wouldn't have defended herself, but um, I heard a lot of things about her anyway. Then I moved to North Carolina and then I heard the same thing and I was just kind of like, "I guess the same girl goes to all these schools," and you know, so, I don't know.

As I got into junior high I heard the crazy "true" story of the girl who masturbated with a hot dog. Once I reached high school, the legends surrounding masturbation had reached all new heights. I heard the "real" story of a girl who got caught "playing Barbies" by a friend who was spending the night at her house. Presumably the hot dog story had been heard enough so this was the new version. Buffy, we'll call her, was using Barbie to masturbate with, although it is unclear if she was just stimulating herself or actually penetrating herself vaginally. Either way, this story was with our class until the day we graduated.

When I was in junior high one of my classmates told us the story of a girl who was caught masturbating with a frozen frank. I remember being told this in the sixth grade after gym class. She said it happened only a few years earlier in the gym's locker room. The girl was caught by the gym teacher and had to visit the principal who then made her tell her parents. I completely believed the story. I even thought it could have been one of my brother's friends because he was three years older. We did think it was very sick and disgusting.

While the hot dog is the most commonly used item in the junior high legends, cucumbers become the folkloric dildo of choice for later ages, as in the circulated lists of "Reasons Women Prefer Cucumbers to Men," for example, cucumbers stay hard for a week; a cucumber will always respect you in the morning; a cucumber never leaves the toilet seat up. So strong is the association that one student reported that a friend who was a waitress was sent in a kitchen emergency to the grocery store to buy one cucumber and blushed the whole way there and back.

It is not surprising that girls in early adolescence tell these stories, given that they are at an age at which there is relative discomfort about sexuality and a lack of knowledge about sexual anatomy, particularly the vagina. Young men might also find this story believable because they both assume female masturbation would involve inserting a penis substitute and have their own misunderstandings about vaginal capacity.

Although these stories demonstrate a lack of understanding of anatomy on the part of adolescents, it should be pointed out that even adults use some basic vocabulary incorrectly, referring to the vagina when they actually mean the vulva (the external genitalia), and have their own misunderstandings. The vagina is incorrectly viewed by many people as a long tube having set dimensions, with an individual woman's vagina always being the same size. In fact, the vagina is best described as "potential space" which can expand or contract in different physiological states and in response to childbirth, intercourse, etc. (Sloane, 1993). Even if people are told more about the vagina, such as Sloane's description below, they may still have a fear that "potential space" is also uncharted space:

> The size of the vagina is so variable and so capable of distension that it is difficult to measure its dimensions. . . . Actually, the tube of the vagina is only a potential space, because its anterior and posterior walls are thrown up into transverse folds that are in close apposition. (Sloane, 1993, p. 38)

When girls first learn about tampons, they may be embarrassed to articulate their fear that these objects can disappear into that unknown and vast space. They also may believe that tampons can go beyond the vagina and disappear into the uterus. After all, they may reason, if a baby can come out of a uterus, surely a tampon can get in. They may even know that the cervix, with its small opening, the os, lies between the body of the uterus and the vagina. However, they may not realize that the opening is extremely small, "about the diameter of a very thin straw" under normal circumstances (that is, until childbirth, after which it will remain *slightly* enlarged) (Boston Women's Health Book Collective, 1998, p. 274). While the anxiety about migrating tampons may not be expressed through direct questions, it certainly appears in the numerous tampon-related stories:

> A tale I heard several times under different circumstances but more when I was in high school. This girl was taken to the hospital because she had put too many tampons in. She wanted to go to a party and not worry about putting any in her purse.

> A woman goes to the doctor, concerned because she feels lumps around her groin and she thinks they might be cysts. She goes to the doctor and he pulls not one, not two, but three lost tampons out of her.

> My roommate told me a story that a friend told her who supposedly heard it from a doctor. There was a girl who came into the emergency room one night because her stomach didn't feel right. When the doctor examined her, he found that she had lost 5 tampons in her vagina.

The idea of lost tampons feeling like lumps in the groin or causing a girl's stomach to feel bad indicates that the entire internal anatomy is a mystery to the storytellers.

The view of the vagina as huge and engulfing appears in jokes and stories about the "vagina infinita." For example, a bawdy folksong, referring to a woman of "large dimension," tells how the entire soccer team went in last night and "none has yet come out of it." Folklore depicts the vagina as capable of being of enormous size, in which anything might become lost or stored. Several jokes illustrate this view of the vagina:

> A man is wandering around in a woman's vagina with a flashlight. He runs into another man who says, "If you'll lend me your flashlight, I can find my car keys and we can drive out of here."

> A woman went to her OB/GYN and he was examining her and he said, "What a hole!" "What a hole!" and she said, "You didn't have to say it twice," and he said, "I didn't. The second one was an echo."

> A woman went to her OB/GYN and he was examining her and he was talking about how big her vagina was so when she got home she got a mirror and went into the bathroom, sat on the floor, and was looking at herself so her husband came to tell her something and said, "Damn, don't fall in that hole in the floor."

According to legend, other objects besides tampons and hot dogs have been lost in vaginas. There is one story of a cheerleader who does a big leap and split and five class rings fall out. This story goes back to the image of the promiscuous cheerleader (see Chapter 6) as the woman who will try to satisfy large numbers of men—especially athletes—for her own pleasure. It can only be assumed that she was wearing nothing that would have kept the rings from falling out, which feeds into a pornographic fantasy image—the cheerleader with no underwear.

When folklore classes have studied Mexican-American legends about various wormlike creatures (vaginal serpents) crawling up into a woman and spawning in her so that she appears pregnant, students dismiss the serpent as unbelievable but express concern about whether bugs could crawl into the vagina and get into the uterus. However, one student submitted this story:

My mother was an assistant to an OB/GYN—obstetrician/gynecologist. She worked with a nurse who told her this story:

I was in the emergency room one night when this couple came in. The woman was quite shaken up. They had been camping and during the night, a snake had crawled into the woman's sleeping bag. She slept with no underwear on, and the snake crawled up inside her. She felt this happening but couldn't get it out. Her husband took her to the ER to remove the snake. I don't know how they got it out. Maybe they lured it out with a mouse.

Students have not turned in a lot of lore involving insects which crawl into the vagina, though there is the story of the tick that stops menstruation, cited in Chapter 4, and the following stories which give a message about the dangerous breeding ground that a woman's vagina can be, an issue discussed later in this chapter:

I told my best friend that I was going to the gynecologist. She began sharing her own experience at the gynecologist and then told me about this girl whose mom is a gynecologist. One day this nasty, unclean lady went in for a check-up. As the doctor was examining her, baby spiders began crawling out of the woman. The doctor was so disgusted she had to change profession.

Janet (I work with her in the ER) told me a horrendous story. They had a no-insurance case come in late one night with a distended abdomen. They couldn't find anything in X-ray so they wheeled her in for emergency surgery. They put her under and as they cut into her lower pelvic region, a swarm of roaches flew into the OR. I've never heard of this happening before and don't even know if it's medically possible. Supposedly, every night she would douche and lay her douche bag in the sink. (I guess because she was low income she re-used the same bag—gross!) The roaches would crawl across it and laid eggs on the top. They hatched in her cervix. I guess it's true that they like warm, moist places!

Because many do not understand that the cervix, with its very small opening and mucus secretions protecting the opening, can keep out insects, this story seems in the realm of the possible. This is a frightening view, because the vagina and the uterus seem very vulnerable, and the false belief is that once something does get inside, it can easily get lost and, if alive, may multiply. This last story, with its emphasis on the woman being low-income, also reflects stereotypes about poverty and lack of cleanliness.

Folklore about the "vagina dentata," or toothed vagina, though internationally recognized and appearing in earlier American collections, does not seem to be very important or prevalent in the current folklore of the students from whom we collected. One story combines the vagina infinita with the vagina dentata and adds a theme of objects lost through medical incompetence:

My roommate told me this legend—he was convinced it was true. . . . This man took his wife to the doctor, complaining that something sharp and painful was in her vagina when he had sex with her. "There's some kind of monster or animal up there that keeps biting me!" The doctors did exploratory surgery and found a syringe left over from a hysterectomy a few months earlier.

The dual absurdity—that a woman wouldn't notice a syringe in her vagina and that a man would be convinced it was an animal in there—obviously was not enough to tip off at least one person that the story was not true. In another legend, popular during the Vietnam war, the dangerous object in the vagina is intentional:

The story was that there was a group of Vietnamese prostitutes who traveled around Vietnam. These women were equipped rather oddly, for they put a razor blade sunk in gum inside their vaginas before intercourse with an American soldier, killing a few by bleeding, and seriously injuring others. I also heard this as just a warning of women hired by the Viet Cong, but at least two men heard it as a legendary set of women.

This legend could have served several functions: to keep American soldiers away from prostitutes (the function also served by stories of untreatable forms of sexually transmitted diseases), to increase the rage of the military against the Vietnamese, and to demonize even the women, so that there would be no sympathy with civilians. To believe this, someone would have to envision the vagina as a tube that was always open; otherwise, it would be clear that the razor blade would damage the woman very seriously. There are other stories that imply Asian women's genitals are different from those of white women, so this legend may fit into that racist view.

Besides the two stories cited above, the presence of the vagina dentata is strongest in jokes, such as this one:

There was this Baptist minister and he caught his son in the act with the deacon's daughter and really let him have it. That night he got a call from this widow, who was trying to seduce him. She began masturbating with a whiskey bottle which got stuck. When she tried to get it out, it broke in the middle. When he got there, he started right in without waiting and got cut up. Later he apologized to his son and said, "Enjoy it while you can; they get teeth when they get older."

The concept of the vagina dentata may have been relegated primarily to jokes, while fear of the toothless gripping power of a woman's vagina still figures in legends of couples becoming stuck together during intercourse. Students are curious about the nature of the vagina and occasionally are brave enough to ask whether it's true, as jokes indicate, that the vagina gets very loose and gripless with age. This creates a good opportunity to discuss the pubococcygeus muscles (which play a role in vaginal contractions during orgasm, in childbirth, and in control of urination) and of Kegel exercises, which strengthen these muscles. Students may be relieved to know that these muscles, like any muscles, respond to exercise.

Many of the stories in this chapter indicate a common discomfort about contact with the vagina and a general sense of disgust with women's genitals. The legends about masturbation are often associated with one particular girl, either one who does not fit in and is, therefore, seen as unlikely to have a boyfriend or one who has a reputation for being "easy." By focusing on outcast, misfit, low-income, or promiscuous women, these stories serve as a warning about what happens to women and girls if they attempt to control their own sexuality through masturbation. These stories also show how folklore is used as a form of social control, threatening those who do not conform to expected norms with being labeled sexually deviant.

Boys are also warned not to masturbate, though the quickly disproved threats of going blind or growing hair on one's palms versus the legends threatening girls with public and lasting humiliation suggest that here, too, male sexual activity is not only more forgivable but even expected. It is a sign of virility if a man can "jack off" quickly. One reported fraternity initiation rite, which has been identified as a legend, in which the pledges stand around a pizza and the last one to ejaculate on it has to eat it, would suggest a high value given to this sign of potency. The homoerotic implications of this ritual are obvious. Watching other men masturbate is made acceptable by the fraternity brothers' presumed heterosexuality, while stories of the same activity by a group of gay men would undoubtedly be viewed as one more indication of perverted sexuality. We have heard no legends about initiations in which women compete to reach orgasm first through masturbation.

Joycelyn Elders was asked to resign her post as Surgeon General after she suggested that masturbation is a part of human sexuality and possibly should be included in the school curriculum about sexuality. Her statement, given in response to a direct question about masturbation as a form of safer sex, is completely reasonable from both a public health and an educational perspective. This statement was certainly not the sole reason for her departure, since her forced resignation was a highly political move that served to silence a physician who was willing to take controversial and highly principled stands about a number of areas such as sexuality education. The public reaction to her view on masturbation, however, does indicate the way the subject generates immediate and intense responses and suggests an acute discomfort among many people with this topic. One of the goals of education is to correct false beliefs and misunderstandings, so it does seem reasonable that the schools might help students feel they are not sick and abnormal if they masturbate. Surveys about sexuality education in the schools show that the least discussed areas include homosexuality, abortion, and masturbation. If one reason for avoiding the discussion of masturbation is that it might give students "ideas," then those who oppose it are clearly ignoring the fact that masturbation is usually something kids figure out without any help from the schools and also that they are already talking about it in their very commonly circulating folklore. One way discomforts and anxieties are expressed is through legends, and these masturbation stories are bubbling over with concerns and questions that the young women will not directly ask. For example, it is unlikely that a girl will ask an adult directly if women really masturbate with hot dogs and if they can really get stuck; however, by telling the story to friends, they can all discuss the taboo topic, pooling whatever opinions and information, however misinformed, they may have. These stories of women and girls who need emergency room treatment for removal of hot dogs, while certainly misrepresenting the way a majority of women masturbate (clitoral stimulation is more of a focus than vaginal penetration), also spell out a socially sanctioned warning to women who try to take some control of their sexual pleasure through masturbation, especially if it involves a penis-substitute.

If women can find sexual pleasure without men, there is a perceived threat to heterosexual relations. The response to these perceived threats may also be expressed in antagonism toward lesbians. It is interesting that so many attacks on the Clinton administration in its *first* years focused on sexual issues, including the battle over gays in the military, anything Joycelyn Elders said about sexuality education, and rumors about the sexual orientation of several Clinton appointees, as well as about the First Lady herself. For example, there was a joke that circulated the summer after Clinton was elected, when there were serious floods in the Midwest:

Q: Why was there so much flooding in the Midwest?
A: Because Hillary took all the dykes to Washington.

Of course, one reason Hillary Rodham Clinton, a strong professional woman, was identified as a lesbian, or at least as having many lesbian friends, was in order to present Clinton as a weak, ineffectual president whose decisions were really controlled by his wife. There were also jokes about Hillary Clinton that implied she was more "man" than her husband, such as the following:

Hillary went to the doctor for an examination and returned home in an unusually good mood. She said, "Bill, the doctor told me I have the breasts of a 37-year-old." Bill replied, "What did he say about your 49-year-old pussy?" She said, "Oh, we didn't talk about you."

During Clinton's second term as president, much of the country focused on his extramarital sexual activity. The use of jokes to focus the discussion appears, for example, in a joke previously and variously told about Joan Collins, Madonna, blondes, and sorority sisters (demonstrating the great adaptability of jokes) and with greater piquancy in 1998 because of the recent release of the movie *Titanic*:

Q: What's the difference between Clinton and the Titanic?
A: We know how many people went down on the Titanic.

In general, the jokes emphasized oral sex and titillating details from the Starr Report. Some of these attacks seem contradictory. If Clinton is less of a man because his wife is so strong, then how is his alleged behavior as the man whose libido rages out of control explained? Nor is this the only contradiction. At the same time jokes focused on Clinton's promiscuity, they also portrayed him as sexually incompetent, with the two themes coming together in such jokes as:

They surveyed 100 women in the D.C. area and asked them if they were given the opportunity, would they sleep with Bill Clinton. Ten women said no way, 15 said they would consider it, and the other 75 said never again.

By emphasizing his lack of sexual skill (no one wants to repeat a sexual encounter with him), Clinton's detractors undermine one stereotypical marker of male success—many conquests—that otherwise might have been seen as to his credit. Male success, often identified with sexual prowess, is also popularly marked by "having" sexually attractive women—the image of the successful man with a beautiful young woman draped on each arm. Thus follows the common practice of attacking men by attacking "their" women. From the very beginning of Clinton's administration, attacks on his politics have been couched in jokes about Clinton's manhood, often by denigrating his wife. The same kinds of jokes that were used against Clinton can be turned against any "enemy," even the rival football team (*Why does the {rival college} team still play on a grass field? They need somewhere for the cheerleaders to graze),* thus simultaneously creating negative views of the "enemy" and reinforcing certain expectations of what "real" men and women are like.

Women and Pets

Another group of circulating legends goes one step further in reducing women's need for men in order to have sexual pleasure: women having sex with household pets. There is a female version of the gerbil story (not nearly as common as the one about a gerbil in a man's rectum story) such as the following, reported by a young woman who had heard it at a baby shower:

Ya'll, did you hear about the girl in Savannah and the gerbil? Oh my God! This woman, I guess to get her thrills, stuck a tube—a long plastic tunnel-like thing—into her—you know (gestures at her vaginal area) . . . her hole and gets her pet gerbil and puts it into the tube and the gerbil crawled up the tube and went into her (whispers) pussy and wiggles around and makes her feel good. (Shouts) But the gerbil got stuck! She had to go to the hospital to get them to take it out.

However, much more common are the stories of surprise parties that catch a woman in the act of sex with a pet. There are a number of variants of these stories, involving various foods and occasions:

A woman in her thirties was planning to get married for the first time, and her friends were excited that it was finally happening. So they were going to give a surprise shower for her. Her fiancé knew that when she went to work each morning, she would lock her dog Bruno in the basement, and when she got home at 6:00, the first thing she would do is go down to the basement and let Bruno out. So the fiancé opened the house (he had a key), and the lady friends decorated the basement and hid there awaiting the bride-to-be's return.

About 6:00 they heard her come in the front door, after which she stayed upstairs awhile, going back and forth into the kitchen, etc. A few minutes later, she opened the basement door and started down the stairs, calling Bruno, telling him she had a treat for him. About that time, somebody turned on the lights and everyone shouted "Surprise!" There stood the bride-to-be naked, with peanut butter covering her breasts and genitals.

Needless to say, the wedding was called off.

Some of the stories, collected from students and also discussed in *Foaf-Tale News* (October, 1994), involve a surprise birthday party thrown by a roommate and attended by co-workers. In one version, the woman leaves town and her final check is mailed to her. Whipped cream is sometimes the food of choice, instead of peanut butter. All these stories were attached to a specific place and were told by someone in the twice-removed relationship common to contemporary legends. One version added some interesting details to the description of the woman:

> There's this twenty-something female bank clerk who shares her apartment with another woman. Although attractive, she never has time to date or go out because of unusual constraints of her job. Her roommate somehow discovers that the clerk's birthday is impending, and manages to gather the clerk's few friends and get them to the apartment for a surprise party. (Fleming, 1994, p. 10)

The legend continues with the same story of the peanut butter smeared in her crotch as a treat for her pet dog. In terms of the sexual needs of women and whether those can be fulfilled without men, these legends raise interesting issues. The variant that involves a woman who does not have time to date because of work can be examined in several ways. It may be a negative comment about women who succeed in the work-place, who either find dogs adequate substitutes for men when they are too busy to date, or possibly use work as an excuse not to date because their dogs keep them satisfied. In either case, working women are viewed as perverted in their sexuality. In the variants in which the surprise party is thrown by her fiancé, the woman clearly has a man but seems to prefer a dog, which is even more threatening to men. It should be noted that versions of this story are told by both men and women. In another version, the woman is clearly described as one who could not get a man, which makes the story less threatening to men than one about a woman who is actually engaged to be married:

> There was this one secretary in a big office who no one liked. She was absolutely hideous, she never got dates, never went out, she had no life except work. No one usually talked to her because she was so ugly, but she was a good secretary.

In discussions of this legend, women have offered other interpretations, such as that men are "beasts" and so are dogs. One woman questioned that since a woman gets the same thing from a man and a dog—a physical relationship and sexual satisfaction, with no emotion—what's the difference? Another suggested that the stories about professional women show women becoming more like men; they are choosing sexual gratification without romance, love, or conversation. These interpretations by women identify the behavior of men, rather than that of women, as problematic.

Changes and developments in a legend or series of related legends can be very instructive in pointing out changing attitudes and concerns. Consider, for example, the immediate precursor to the "peanut butter surprise," a legend sometimes referred to as the "surpriser surprised":

> It was this (teenage) girl's birthday and she was going to celebrate it with her parents at their summer cottage. They had already left; she stayed behind to do the laundry and was then going to drive over with her boyfriend. Anyway, her boyfriend came over and they were upstairs having sex, when she remembered she had to switch the laundry from the washer to the drier. So he carried her piggyback down the stairs and they

were naked and laughing . . . And they went to the basement
and turned on the light and all these people jumped out yelling
"Surprise!"—her parents and everyone. They had come to give
her a surprise party. She was so embarrassed. I think the whole
family left town and put her in another school.

Oh, oh, the surprise party thing. This happened to a friend of
my roommate's my freshman year, I mean, it happened, I'm
pretty sure it happened to her. . . . She had gone home for the
weekend and it was her birthday. And her parents had told her
that they were really sorry but she was an adult and they just
figured she could be there by herself or whatever and she's just
like all for it. And so she went home anyway. And, you know,
she's a college student and, of course, she's got a lot of laundry.
So she's doing her laundry at the same time when her boyfriend
came over and they were having sex in her parents' bedroom
which was upstairs and, uh, they heard a noise downstairs so
they figured, "Well, we might as well, you know, go and change
out the laundry or whatever." So he's giving her a piggyback
ride down the stairs. There's a surprise party downstairs for the
girl. You know they're piggybacking down the stairs naked.

In this legend, the problem, apart from the obvious one of embarrassment at being caught naked, is that the couple has been engaging in
premarital sex. In the 1950s and 1960s, the legend was told with the
young couple being engaged (Brunvand, 1981); in the 1980s, students
mostly reported it with a high school or college age couple and no mention of an engagement. This slight variation may reflect a growing acceptance of premarital sex between those already committed to each
other but still some concern about it for the unattached. By the mid-
1990s, while the embarrassment at being caught nude remained, there
seemed to be little shock value left in the premarital sex. Now it takes
a woman satisfying herself without a man and bestiality to provide
enough "surprise" to shock us.

Legends reflect and reveal the moving boundaries of what is acceptable or distressing to society. Inappropriate sexual intercourse is often punished in legend by the couple becoming stuck together; allegedly there is a spasm and they become locked together, unable to pull apart, which is referred to as "penis captivus" (Brunvand, 1984, 142–45). There are strong muscles surrounding the vagina which can be contracted voluntarily or involuntarily (during orgasm) and can be strengthened by pelvic floor muscle exercises (Kegel exercises). Some women experience vaginismus, in which there is a strong, involuntary contraction or spasm of the vaginal muscles. However, rather than trapping a penis, it is more likely to prevent penetration by making it too difficult. The "punishment" of being locked together has remained constant for over six centuries, but the "sin" has changed with the times. In the fourteenth century, a legend reported a *married* couple punished for intercourse because they were doing it too close to the church—the couple became stuck to each other. In the modern version of the legend, it takes a lot more than simple proximity to a church for divine retribution to come into play. For example, two African American students reported legends from their Baptist churches. In one story a gay couple having intercourse in one of the pews became stuck together. In the other, it was a heterosexual couple, but they were going one step further in their sacrilegious behavior, since they were having intercourse on the altar. In other variants, proximity to a church is not the issue. Adultery is also punishable no matter where it takes place. The following story told by a Korean-American woman is a perfect example of the theme of punishment of adultery by fusion:

> I remembered today that my mother had told me this story long time ago. Supposedly in Korea, there was this incident in which a sister-in-law was sleeping with her sister's husband. Well, they lived in the same house as is often the case in Korea, or Asian societies, and one day, the father walked in when the sister-in-law and the husband were having sex. Well, they were in

so much shock that they were stuck together and they had to be taken to the hospital. Stuck together, I don't know how they moved around!

In the United States, there is a common story about a couple in the back seat of a car who become locked together after being startled by a patrolling police officer and who then have to be taken to the emergency room to be separated. In this case, being sexually active in a public space is the precipitating factor. Among children and younger teenagers, for whom the most preliminary sexual activity has crossed a boundary, there are legends about couples locking braces while kissing, an important warning among certain groups for whom necking is still a big step.

Returning to the "peanut butter surprise legends," listeners tend to be disgusted by the involvement of the dog, by the bestiality. However, while the thought of a woman engaging in bestiality truly disturbs them, when presented with folklore about male bestiality they respond with knowing laughter rather than "Ew, gross." Bestiality is a fairly standard folkloric assumption about certain groups of men (such as sheep shearers, shepherds, and frat boys), with jokes told about:

rival agricultural schools:

Q: Why did the Ag student marry his cow?
A: Because he had to.

neighboring rival states:

Q: How do you practice safe sex in Alabama?
A: Put an "X" on the cows that kick.

the current national enemy:

Q: Why don't they have driver's ed and sex ed on the same day in Iraqi schools?
A: Because it's too hard on the camel.

men in general:

Q: Why did God create women?

A: Because sheep can't cook.

or different ethnic groups and nationalities:

Q: Why do Scotsman wear kilts?

A: Because sheep can hear a zipper a mile away.

When several students mentioned, for example, intercourse with a fraternity's mascot goat as an initiation rite, no one seemed particularly shocked. At a man's twenty-first birthday party, his friends paid for a "rent-a-sheep" as his gift, clearly drawing on a shared understanding about young men and animals (for those who are worried about the sheep in this true story, the worst that happened was that it ate a large part of the garden). The common understandings that underlie these jokes fit in with the view that "men will screw anything." The point here is not a call for equal rights in bestiality but that once again our folklore and the responses to it reveal a double standard. Men are expected to be highly sexually active and experimental. Even though the jokes are often used to insult a particular group, the behavior is still seen as within a "normal" range, as long as men play an insertive role (because men play a receptive role in the gerbil stories, that behavior is considered abnormal); usually there are no punishments for men who have sex with sheep. We came across a rare exception in one telling of a legend about a man having intercourse with a cat; the cat dies and he has to go to the emergency room to remove the stuck cat. However, we found nothing comparable to the numerous versions of the peanut butter surprise story, told with great detail and emphasizing the humiliation of the woman. It is interesting that even though the peanut butter surprise story does not involve penetration, it is seen as a more serious violation than a man having intercourse with an animal. Women are expected to be less sexually daring and not to violate the very important boundary by having sex without men; sex with an animal results in humiliation or worse. For example, the one piece of information many people can cite about Catherine the Great is the false story that she was crushed to death while having intercourse with a horse.

The Dirty and Disgusting "Down There"

These peanut butter surprise stories show disgust for oral-vulval sex as something dirty (something only a dog would do and then only with food as an inducement) and also disgust that some women may prefer oral sex to whatever other sexual activities are available to them, presumably including intercourse. This tension between the notion that women prefer receiving oral sex while men dislike giving it appears in other forms. For example, there was a bumper sticker and a joke that circulated in Louisiana: "Cajuns make better lovers; they'll eat anything." There are undoubtedly cultural variations in preference, but in the folklore we've collected, women's vulvas are assumed to be so unappealing that no one would normally want to have oral contact with one, except dogs and Cajuns, both of whom are noted for having odd culinary tastes. Even some of the sexual self-help books and manuals suggest using foods such as whipped cream to make oral sex more appealing, so using food for enticing a dog is not surprising.

A group of women suggested that perhaps this story is a reflection of women's enjoyment of oral sex and their lack of satisfaction in getting enough pleasure this way because men are viewed as so averse to cunnilingus. This interpretation may be borne out by another group of legends which focus on food used to make oral sex more appealing, with disastrous consequences:

It's just a story. It's really gross about this girl and this guy. This girl's sex life with this boyfriend hasn't really been exciting, so she decided that she would somehow spice up her sex life. And her boyfriend liked tuna fish, and she spread it all over her body. When her boyfriend came home, she was sitting there waiting for him. Well, he came home, and he ate all the tuna fish and did whatever. And anyway, so like a couple of weeks later, she was having like incredible stomach pains and she just couldn't eat, and she could barely talk, and she was throwing up everything. She went to the doctor and they couldn't find out what was wrong. So she went to the gynecologist. And the gynecologist checked her out, and when he had finished checking her out, he stepped away from her, leaned over, and puked in the trash can that was sitting there. And um, she was like, "Great—what, what is wrong?" So he asked her if she had been doing anything kinda weird lately, and she said, "Well actually, you know me and my boyfriend made tuna fish," and she told him the whole story. And he said, "Well, didn't you know that tuna is a meat, and if you leave it out, it attracts maggots." And she had maggots in her uterus and her stomach lining and her ovaries. All the maggots were because they had nothing else to eat. And that's why it had eaten away half her uterus and stuff like that. But I don't think it's true because maggots come from flies. They have to be sitting out.

One woman reported that she had heard this story told about the first time a young man was going to try oral sex and his partner's attempt to make it easier and more appealing. Women get punished in these stories for attempting to find pleasure outside vaginal-penile intercourse. Of course, this might be taken as a healthy warning about not leaving foreign objects or matter in the vagina, but it seems more connected to disgust for oral sex or a comment on women's innate dirtiness. In these legends vaginas are dirty, disgusting places, which not only smell bad but, like garbage pails, can also breed maggots. The legend, in addition to portraying oral sex as an abhorrent and unacceptable deviance and the vagina as innately dirty, shows once again that when it comes to sexual experimentation, even when a man is equally involved, it is the woman alone who is punished, as this variant emphasizes:

A girl and her boyfriend were having oral sex when the guy decided it would be fun to put peanut butter on himself. A fly got stuck in the peanut butter, and, of course, the girl swallowed the fly. Later that week she was taken to the hospital with a terrible stomachache. When her stomach was pumped, they discovered maggots in her stomach.

A variant combines the cunnilingus story with the animal motif (Stu, 1994). In this case the tuna fish is placed in her vagina so her cat can lick it out. The choice of tuna fish makes sense for the cat story in terms of cats' food preferences but, in the ones about boyfriends, the choice seems to represent what some men think about women's genitals—that they smell fishy—as expressed in many jokes:

Q: What did the blind man say as he passed the fish market?
A: Good morning, girls.

Q: Why don't they let women swim in the ocean anymore?
A: They can't get the smell out of the fish.

It is certainly not just men who think vulvas are fishy-smelling, as can be seen in these jokes collected about lesbians (though it was not clear whether all the informants were lesbians):

Q: What do you call a blind lesbian in a fish market?
A: Dazed and confused.

Q: What is an open can of tuna fish in a lesbian's apartment called?
A: Potpourri.

Q: What do Polish lesbians use for lubricant?
A: Tartar sauce.

If lesbians tell the last joke, it is another example of the ease with which one marginalized group may exhibit prejudice toward another.

Another legend draws on the theme of food in the vagina, but with an obvious racist addition:

I heard this story told by a girl who was a candy striper at St. Mary's hospital here in Athens. One night an old black lady came into the emergency room and reported that "somethin' is growin' out of my vagism." When the doctor examined her he discovered she had used a potato peel as a contraceptive sponge. She had left it and one of the eyes had sprouted. This was told as factual.

Another story reports that a woman went to the doctor with something green growing out of her vagina. It turns out that her husband had put a potato peel in her to keep her faithful.

Vaginas and vulvas are seen as being associated with both food and infection in the following jokes:

Q: What do you call an anorexic with a yeast infection?
A: A quarter pounder with cheese.

Q: Did you hear about that poor Jewish girl?
A: She couldn't go to the Seder because she had a yeast infection.

The latter joke depends upon the knowledge that only unleavened products—that is, involving no yeast or rising agent—may be eaten during Passover, the holiday during which the Seder, a special holiday meal and service, is held. Given all the food imagery associated with women's sexuality (from cheesecake to her melon breasts and cherry, to her having buns in the oven, and she herself being a peach, a tomato, a cookie, a honey) and the sexual metaphor of "eating," it is not surprising that food plays such a large role in legendry dealing with women's sexuality, nor that the food spoils when women fail to follow society's (sexual) recipes.

A story, which circulated by e-mail in early 2000, but which we have only heard once in an oral form (and in that case referring directly to the e-mail) combines many themes in this chapter: punishment of women for masturbation, food in the vagina, live animals used for sexual pleasure, the vagina as a breeding place for the growth of disgusting organisms, and homophobia. The legend is presented as a news story with a specific location and name for the victim. In summary, a woman, while watching lesbian pornography, masturbated in the bath tub using a live lobster. The next day she experienced horrible pains and passed large numbers of baby mud shrimp from her vagina; the explanation is that the lobster defecated the mud shrimp eggs into her vagina. Seeing the toilet full of thousands of mud shrimp, she went into shock and fell, dying of head trauma and shock.

From these stories it would be hard to guess that vaginas are self-cleaning organs. It is certainly possible that if a tampon or other foreign body were left in the vagina too long, irritation or infection could occur. However, secretions from the cervix and vagina, combined with normal shedding of mucosal cells, help keep the vagina clean. Because of a commonly held belief in the United States that the vagina is inherently dirty and smells bad, many women douche to clean and perfume the vagina. Douching is associated with pelvic inflammatory disease and ectopic pregnancy, possibly because organisms are forced into the upper reproductive tract. False beliefs about the vagina can, therefore, lead to poor health.

Putting together the information gleaned from legends, jokes, and other folklore, the vagina would be described as an area that smells bad, in which things can easily get stuck or lost, and in which cockroaches, maggots, and mud shrimp can easily breed. With all the stories that make vaginas seem so disgusting, there is a legend that takes a slightly different turn:

Well, I went to see the dentist to get my teeth cleaned and after the cleaning he came and checked and he started to turn and leave, and then he came back and he said, "Now, I'm gonna tell you a story. I probably shouldn't tell you this story, 'cause we don't know who the lady is, and one of these days I'm gonna tell this story to somebody, it's gonna be the lady and she's gonna be embarrassed." Embarrassment being a part of the story. And I asked what it was about, of course, and he said that there was a woman here— There's a lady here in town. Her momma came over from Alabama for Thanksgiving. She wanted to see her grandchildren and just visit. They were havin' a real nice time. Then momma said, "Oh but I've gotta cut it short, and the reason I've gotta cut it short is I have an appointment for a check-up with my gynecologist." "Oh," said her daughter, "don't you worry, momma. I can just set you up right here. You can go to my gynecologist." So that's what they decided to do. Well, the day came for the check-up and after she got through, Momma came out and got in the car with her daughter and they were driving home, and Momma said, "Well, I just can't believe that you go to that man. He is so unprofessional. I was just so shocked you could have anything to do with anybody like that." Her daughter said, "What are you talkin' about, momma?" "Oh," said Momma, "we go,—I was on the table and he came in and he lifted up that sheet and he looked under and he said, 'Mm! Fancy!'" Well the daughter didn't know what that was all about, so said, "Now, Momma, are you sure that's what he said? Are you sure that's what happened?" "It certainly is," said Momma. "He looked under that sheet and he said, 'Mm! Fancy!'" And then, the daughter—I can't remember what comes next— the daughter says, "Well, now, Momma, did you do anything?" "No, I didn't do anything. How dare you ask me that?" "Are you sure you didn't have some perfume on?" "I certainly did not. All I had was some of that feminine hygiene spray, that deodorant you have in the guest bathroom." Well, the daughter knew she didn't have any feminine hygiene deodorant in the guest bath-room, so when she got home, she went and checked. And when she had been doing crafts and things for Thanksgiving, she had

left a little spray can of gold glitter paint in the guest bathroom. And now, the daughter is so embarrassed, she won't go see the gynecologist. And that's the story.

Because many women accept the perception of women's genitals as dirty and disgusting, it is not surprising, or, in fact, uncommon, that a woman would douche or use a feminine deodorant spray before seeing a gynecologist. She is uncomfortable with her own genitals and does not want to offend the doctor with the smell; the idea that this product might interfere with the exam or mask some problem is obviously not a concern. The rest of the story, which has circulated widely in a number of variations, is a new version of many of the classic stories, real or legendary, about mixing up products (glue instead of nose drops; SuperGlue instead of eye drops). Unlike those stories, the end result, rather than being physically painful or damaging, is humiliating. (The woman who told this version above particularly enjoyed the idea of being able to get a gynecology appointment at short notice, a detail that reduced the credibility of the legend for her.)

A precursor of this legend is the one in which a woman en route to the gynecologist stops at a public restroom, where, because there is no toilet paper, she has to use tissue grabbed from her purse. Some Green Stamps entangled in the tissue stick to her without her realizing it. When the doctor examines her, he comments, "I didn't know they were giving these out these days." The woman, of course, is embarrassed, though whether laughingly or to the point of mortification varies with the telling. Here the woman's embarrassment results from trying to make her genitals more pleasant in a far more basic way—one last bathroom trip and wipe, but these adult women's stories along with the teenagers' stories of menstrual periods starting with embarrassing unexpectedness suggest not only a woman's discomfort with her own body but also a disconnectedness to the point of not really knowing what's going on "down there."

This lack of knowledge of our own bodies can have serious effects, so that we don't know when something is really wrong (if women's genitals are usually disgusting, what's one more smelly discharge?) or suffer unnecessary fears (not using tampons because they may disappear) or avoid practices that are certainly harmless and may have some benefits such as masturbation. But there are other risks. Many groups internalize society's negative views of them, so that we may talk about "internalized anti-Semitism" or "internalized homophobia." It would be easy to internalize the gynephobia reflected in much of the folklore in this chapter. The material we have described provides an almost unrelentingly negative view of women's genitals and sexuality, which could easily have an impact on girls' and women's self-esteem. It is hard to have a positive view of your body and sexuality if you don't know much and what you have heard is mostly negative.

Women's movements, particularly women's health movements, have done a great deal to demystify women's anatomy and physiology and to create a much higher level of comfort with our bodies. In the 1970s, many women found that learning to do pelvic self-exams was a powerful experience. We finally learned what was going on under the sheet in the gynecologist's office and we learned to distinguish what was healthy and normal from what might be a health problem. Women's health classes and books explained exactly what went on during a pelvic exam and helped women feel much more positive about our own anatomy. Now many health care practitioners offer women mirrors so they can observe their own genitals and cervixes.

Unfortunately, it seems that much of what we learned has not filtered down, with the result that many adolescents are not getting the information they need. While sexuality education classes usually cover reproductive anatomy and physiology, they often leave out some topics, such as the role of the clitoris (or even what and where it is). One of the topics that is routinely left out of such classes is the pelvic exam. Providing the basic information on what to expect during a pelvic exam could make the initial experience (and subsequent experiences) a lot more comfortable. Being aware of folklore can help direct a teacher to some very important issues that may not be found in a standard syllabus but that are real concerns. For example, it is important to make it clear that tampons cannot "disappear" in, though they may be hard to get out of, the vagina. Discussing how vaginal health and cleanliness are naturally maintained, and what can interfere with that process (such as douching), can help dispel some of the discomfort about vaginal odors. Students often enjoy collecting and critiquing advertisements for vaginal "hygiene" products after these discussions; they might especially appreciate some historical ads as well, such as those promoting Lysol as a douche. Men need to hear the same information so that views of women's sexuality and bodies are not shaped by locker room jokes. In a university women's health course, at the beginning of the class, the professor has students practice saying words such as vagina out loud to each other and then constructing sentences using this vocabulary. Even a seemingly small step such as this increases the comfort level and helps students learn to talk directly about their bodies, health, and sexuality. As they encounter the kind of folklore presented in this chapter, both women and men who have had a positive educational experience related to these topics will be able to recognize and counter the negative views it presents of women's bodies and sexuality.

8

THE FRAT BOY'S SISTER AND THE CHAT ROOM DATE

Incest, Accidental and Otherwise

❏

There was a guy in this frat who brought his younger sister to Athens for a weekend. The frat was having a big party and he thought she'd enjoy it.

The party came, and bro and sis were hanging out, getting really ripped. Sis excused herself to go to the john. A good while later, she had not yet returned, so bro went to look for her.

While stumbling around the frat house, completely soused, he happened upon a room full of guys, "enjoying" some poor girl who was apparently too sick to worry about it, because her head was stuck out the window and it sounded like she was throwing up. Bro joins in the fun.

When everyone has had their turn, they pull the girl, who has passed out, back into the room. Bro realizes with horror that he has just participated in gang-raping his sister.

Many legends are particularly bizarre and improbable, though, by definition, they have to be at least possible and plausible to some listeners. The basic plot of the gang-rape of a drunken woman does seem plausible to those who have read about gang-rapes in college settings, particularly fraternities, while the bizarre aspect is provided by the unintentional incest. There are some minor variations in the story, but all end with the same terrible revelation:

> At a fraternity party, a girl drank too much and passed out leaning out the window. One of the fraternity brothers came into the room and saw her. He lifted up her dress and violated her. When he was done, he went and retrieved one of his friends from the party. He brought his friend into the room, and his friend violated the woman also. They decided to see who she was and so they pulled her in. They looked at her face and the second frat boy said, "Oh my God, that's my sister!"

This legend is told by and to both men and women, especially in late high school or early college, but the message differs for the two groups. Women are warned against the dangers of drinking and attending fraternity parties. Men are either warned to check the identity of a woman before raping her (to look before they rape) or, we hope, reminded that every woman who is raped is somebody's sister—or daughter or mother. One male student interpreted it as "This legend may be anti-rape. It casts the rapist as a typical date rapist. The fledgling rapist (the pledge) is shown the error of his ways by committing rape on a family member."

This legend is widespread nationally and even informants in Australia knew it, with the locale being a party but not a fraternity. Some students reported having heard variations of this legend frequently in high school, so perhaps, as the roommate legend served to warn young men to protect themselves from the imagined dangers of predatory gay men, these stories may serve to warn young women about the real dangers of alcohol as associated with sexual assault. For young women, the horror is in the gang-rape of a woman too drunk to resist; for young men it seems to be the revelation of the identity of the victim. Given that some studies have shown that sexual assault does occur disproportionately in fraternities (Sanday, 1990) and also that college women are often drunk when sexually assaulted, the story may be an effective and important warning.

While the story may serve as a warning about the dangers of alcohol, it also reinforces the false beliefs both that alcohol causes violence and that, because of her drinking, a woman shares guilt in her own rape. Although violence is often associated with alcohol and the interconnections are complex, drinking in itself does not cause violence. People who have committed violence have to be held accountable for their behavior whether or not they have been drinking. There is also a common societal double standard. Women who are hurt when they have been drinking are blamed both for the drinking and for creating the situation in which violence is so easy. On the other hand, men who rape and batter when drinking or drunk are often excused— "it was only the alcohol" or "he's wonderful when he's not drinking." In the versions of the story that clearly state that at least one rapist was drinking ("While stumbling around the frat house, completely soused . . ."), there may be more sympathy for him, because the rape itself is blamed on the alcohol, and the incest, therefore, is seen as even more accidental.

With the introduction into campus life of the "rape pill" (Rohypnol or roofies), an odorless and tasteless drug which can be slipped into a drink, such cautionary tales may be even more important. The drug begins to have an effect within 20–30 minutes, at which point the victims lose motor control and are unable to resist whatever is done to them; the drug also causes amnesia, so the next day they will have no memory of what happened or whom they were with. (The manufacturers of Rohypnol, which is a legitimate prescription medication for severe sleeping disorders [though not sold in the United States, where FDA approval has not been sought], reformulated the drug so that it dissolves more slowly and releases a bright blue color [National Coalition Against Sexual Assault, 1997]; this should help reduce the risk from this particular drug but of course does not eliminate many other ways women can be drugged and raped.)

The Bad Reputation of Fraternities

Fraternities do have a bad reputation in legend and rumor, as well as from cases documented in the news. For example, a news story reported that a young man had to have his testicle removed after damage to it by a "wedgie" (pulling up very hard and suddenly on a man's jockey shorts from behind, so that the penis and testicles become tightly wedged against the body) during a fraternity hazing (*Chronicle of Higher Education,* 1997). One male college student reported several sexual legends about fraternities, including the story of the rape of the sister. In his version, the rape was part of hazing pledges who were all required to have sex with the young woman passed out face down on the bed. He also reported this story told by a young woman:

> There's a certain fraternity in town, they will take a girl that's really drunk and a guy will try to hook up with her, but they will have already planned out what room he will take her into and there will be brothers in the fraternity hiding at the windows and hiding in the lofts and they will watch the guy and girl have sex. The last two girls were freshmen pledges in other sororities. They call it doing a "stadium." I know for a fact that it is true. It didn't happen to me. I know guys that have watched it.

Whether it is true or not is irrelevant in this context (though not to the young women it may have happened to); that it is believable and believed makes it important. Research on fraternities, which involved interviews with fraternity men and with women who dated fraternity men, uncovered similar stories (Boswell and Spade, 1996):

> A brother of mine was hooking up upstairs with an unattractive woman who had been pursuing him all night. He told some brothers to go outside the window and watch. Well, one thing

led to another and they were almost completely naked when the woman noticed the brothers outside. (P. 142)

These stories are also a reminder that, like the masturbation on the pizza initiation story, a lot of the sexual encounters described are a form of homoerotic bonding. The fraternity brothers who are involved in gang rapes and "stadium" sex are performing for each other. In a review of a book about a famous case of the gang-rape of a developmentally disabled young woman by a group of popular high school athletes, the reviewer points out:

> He [the author] might have gone more deeply into the homo-erotic-homophobic bonding rituals of young men in our society, encouraged in the military as much as in sports, which often lead to voyeurism (a favorite sexual activity among college fraternity brothers, incidentally) and sexual predation. . . . (R. Banks, 1997, p. 8)

While the young men who engage in these behaviors would probably be highly offended if they were identified as homosexual, they do choose to have sex in situations in which other men will be watching them and judging their performance. It is interesting that it is seen as "manly" and heterosexual to be in a situation in which men are watching and being watched during sex, while the same men would speak with disgust of the possibility that a gay man might look at them while showering in a dormitory or military barracks or locker room.

The highly sexual atmosphere of fraternities is well established in folklore and tends to form the backdrop, rather than being the focus, for stories. There are a few legends in which the men are punished for their promiscuity or their sexual violence. One story involves a fraternity which had hired a prostitute for all the brothers; now all the members have AIDS. When this legend was told about a fraternity at the University of Georgia in the early 1990s, its credibility was so great that the student newspaper tried to open the records of the University office overseeing fraternities.

Another legend about fraternities and rape gives a very different view of the victim from the stories of the rape of the sister:

> **It is said that 15 boys in the Pike fraternity date-raped a single girl. In order to keep the girl quiet, the fraternity offered her money. The girl asked for a Corvette instead of the money. She got the car and did not press charges.**

The student reporting this said that he had heard this story told about Pikes at a number of different schools and pointed out that the car is always a Corvette. His comment on the story was that "at least the story tells girls to be wary of frat boys (Pikes in general), but then it teaches boys that girls can be bought—not good." In contrast to the previous legend, this trivializes rape by implying that any harm can be rectified by paying off the woman. She becomes a high-paid prostitute rather than a victim of a crime. The Pikes become the "victims" as they have to come up with enough money for a Corvette. In another version, the fraternity pays her full scholarship to another university. Of course the rape of the sister legend can also be read as one in which the man ultimately suffers—by the pain of recognizing he has raped his sister. Since, in at least some versions of the story, she is unconscious, she need never *know* that anything happened.

Other Unintentional Incest

There also is folklore, going back at least to the story of Oedipus, about unintentional incest that is not necessarily connected with violence, as this legend illustrates:

> **Once there was a freshman guy at a large university. He and his friends went out drinking one night and he ended up going**

home with a girl. After they had sex, he asked her where she was from. She replied that she was from Dallas, Texas. "Oh, really," he said, "I have cousins there." She asked him what their names were, thinking she might know them. He told her their names and she said, "That's my last name!" They figured out they were first cousins. He never slept with anyone on a one-night stand again.

This story was told by freshman men, according to the informant, as a "kind of warning: know last names or at least know your first cousins." In the gang-rape of the sister legend, her identity is concealed because her face is concealed. In this story, seeing the face is no help; it is the "concealed" name that creates the problem. This can be seen as a warning against anonymous sex—sex with strangers may turn out to be a problem if, in fact, they really are not strangers, but relatives. These warnings can be seen in the context of the following views presented by fraternity brothers of faceless, as well as nameless, women who were there for the men's sexual pleasure:

> During these sessions, the brothers we interviewed said that men bragged about what they did the night before with stories of sexual conquests often told by the same men, usually sophomores. The women involved in these exploits were women they did not know or knew but did not respect, or *faceless victims.* Men usually treated girlfriends with respect and did not talk about them in these storytelling sessions. (Boswell and Spade, 1996, p. 138)

Girlfriends, who have faces, names, and *relationships* with fraternity brothers, are considered in a different category, as are sisters, than the anonymous women who can be seduced, abused, or raped, and then treated as fodder for bragging sessions.

Among the serious concerns for health educators and others who work in student services on college campuses are the intertwined issues of alcohol abuse and sexual violence. There are no easy answers, but it is clear that multifaceted approaches are necessary. One way to enter into discussions with both men and women is through their own folklore. By eliciting these legends, it is possible to have men and women discuss together their interpretations of what the messages are about alcohol, anonymous sex, and sex without consent. Discussions may reach the point in which there is consensus that the "nameless" and "faceless" women of the stories are someone's sister—or daughter—and are, in fact, fully human. Even if the realization does not last, there has been a breakthrough that may be more easily attained the next time around.

Incest Narrowly Avoided

In some versions of the fraternity gang-rape, incest is avoided. As one folklorist reported:

> A slightly milder version (which I HAVE heard) of the fraternity legend has the girl being banged on the bed, and the late-arriving participant discovers WHEN his turn comes that it's his sister, i.e., he doesn't actually COMMIT the act (though since his "brothers" do, I reckon it's still incest).

The warning of the dangers of anonymous sex is still here, but for some, the horror of the story may be lessened because the incest—except in a figurative way in that the other frat brothers are committing incest by raping one "brother's" sister—never happens. However, this version may distract the listener from acknowledging the horror of gang-rape of an unconscious woman, because the focus is on the incest that was narrowly avoided, rather than on a gang-rape that did occur.

There are a number of other legends that involve a narrow avoidance of unintentional incest:

OK, there was this young woman studying abroad, in Berlin. Her father, on somewhat short notice, was being sent by his company to Berlin on business. So he thought he'd pay his daughter a surprise visit.

Well, he arrived after dark, and he thought his daughter might be busy studying, so he decided not to contact her till the next morning. After he got checked into his hotel, he wasn't sleepy, so he went out on the town. Specifically, he visited a classy brothel that the bellhop had recommended. He paid his money and was ushered into a small room, to await the arrival of the prostitute who had been assigned to service him.

Imagine his surprise when the door opened and a beautiful young woman exclaimed, "Daddy, what are YOU doing here!"

The sender of this story added, "One can easily imagine a version (though I haven't heard one) in which the lights are so dim that the epiphany doesn't occur until AFTER the encounter." A 1996 made-for-television movie, *The Ultimate Lie,* either drawing on the legend or a shared underlying societal anxiety, was described thus in the listings: "A law school dean discovers the call girl he invited to his hotel room is his daughter." It is interesting that we have not heard legends about father-daughter accidental incest in which the act *actually* occurs. Perhaps it is easier to deal with brother-sister than father-daughter incest. (We should note that in all of the contemporary folklore we've collected, the only instance of mother-son incest appeared in one joke.) This can also be read as a message to men to realize that a prostitute is some *man's* daughter; we hope this father would be horrified if he saw his daughter heading to the bedroom in a brothel with another man. In the fraternity gang-rape story, if we assume the young man was upset by the rape of his sister, whether or not he participated, the message can be seen as rape being wrong because she is *someone's* sister. In either case, men are doing something to women that they would not want other men doing to their own family members.

However, both stories can also be read as placing the blame on the women—one drank too much and passed out; the other chose to work as a prostitute. One older version of the story that clearly places the blame squarely on the man was referred to in a discussion of a cyber-sex story of accidental incest (see below) in *FoafTales News* (Ellis, 1997, p. 13):

> The only place I've seen this story is in an early twentieth or late nineteenth century "white slavery" propaganda tome that Bill Thompson had in his collection of moral panic literature at the University of Reading, England. In that version it's a Victorian epicure whose thing is sex with pre-adolescent girls, whom his contact provides him by kidnaping them off the street. One day he comes into the hotel room provided for the purpose and finds. . . .

The ellipses are the author's but it is clear that it is the "epicure's" own daughter who has been kidnaped. Because it would be hard to blame a pre-adolescent girl for being kidnaped, the tale clearly blames the father. Since it is described as being in a "white slavery" propaganda tome, the message is clearly that this man's behavior puts innocent daughters at risk, as demand creates supply.

Given that these stories depend on initial anonymity, it is not surprising that in the world of electronic communication, where someone's identity can be masked or changed, similar stories would emerge. One current legend is about the risks of that anonymity and ability to change identity:

> A young woman in college is a computer science major and, because she spends all her time at the computer, has little time for a social life. She decides to get into a chat room and hooks up with a guy, with both of them using fake names. Then chat turns to sex and soon they're into cybersex. Eventually, they decide to have real sex and plan a meeting. In order to avoid any

confusion or the need for red carnations, they agree that he'll book a room and they'll both check into it. She gets there first and is waiting in bed naked. The door opens and with horror she recognizes her father.

A version of this (Hathaway, 1997, p. 12) ends with them switching from cybernames to real identities:

> Soon she heard someone walk in and she whispered, "Jeremy." Jeremy said, "Katie?" He turned on the light to see Jen naked in the bed. The next thing heard were two blood-curdling screams. Jen covered herself up and with her most humiliating voice said, "Dad?" and Jeremy said, "JEN!!!"

In an interesting choice of language, this story refers to "her most humiliating voice." This would imply that she is using a tone that will humiliate him. However, in the context, it seems that the term should be "humiliated" because she covers herself up and queries "Dad?" while his response is capitalized and followed by three exclamation points. Since this version is written, it is hard to know how their responses were conveyed. It seems that the "blame" would have to be placed equally but she is the one naked in the bed and, therefore, in a humiliated position.

Another point to raise is the question of whether or not incest occurred. The father and daughter, under assumed names and identities, had been having cybersex, and according to some variants, very kinky cybersex, for a period of time. Just because a physical act did not occur does not mean incest was avoided. One woman, on hearing the story, exclaimed very firmly, "But incest did occur!" Using an analogy, if a man directly described to his daughter sexual activities he would like to engage in with her or if he had phone sex with her, it could be said that incest did occur. Rather than hearing this as a story of incest narrowly avoided, it can be viewed as incest accidentally committed. While this discussion may seem to be technical quibbling, it is important to raise the issue that the incest taboo is more important socially and morally than biologically or even legally. While cybersex between a father and daughter may not fit a legal definition of incest, it certainly fits a "common sense" definition for some.

Cybersex is an area ripe for legends. It has become part of popular culture and even literary works. For example, a book review in *The New York Times Book Review* described the plot of a novel called *Gossip*:

> "Gossip" begins very effectively on a chat line in cyberspace. This particular one is gay, as is our hero, a mild-mannered bookstore clerk name Ralph Eckhart. These chat lines allow perfect anonymity: people invent new identities and switch sexes. One night, while Ralph is chatting with the regulars . . . a stranger enters the "room." (Plunket, 1997, p. 26)

This description could serve as the beginning of any number of sexual legends. A minor subplot of one episode of the television show *Cybill* involved anonymous electronic sexual "chat" between Cybill's younger daughter—a teenager—and her older sister's husband. The sexual cyberchat was played for humor and the daughter used it as a way to one-up her brother-in-law, but the same plot-line could have been spun out very differently with serious consequences. And the risks of such sexual chat rooms are considered great enough to warrant federally funded Internet task forces with the purpose of arresting adults who attempt to arrange to have sex with minors. In recent cases, agents posing as minors in chat rooms have been successful in this goal (Alesia, 1999).

Electronic communication creates possibilities for virtual sex limited only by the imagination of the participants. As such, the lack of limits can create anxieties, such as whether an individual will find out more about herself or himself than she or he wanted to know. Another major anxiety is whether this would lead to a next step—a real physical meeting. If so, there are other sets of anxieties. Would an individual be able to live up to his or her fictional self-creation? Would all those lies about identity be caught? Would the other person be lying? Would "real" sex ever live up to the virtual? Is there danger? Cybersex is supposed to be "safe" sex, but once there is a physical meeting, all the "dangers" of sex joined with the lack of real knowledge about the partner make it very risky.

Incest Jokes as Insults

These legends depend for their effect on an assumed shared abhorrence of incest. Because of this shared set of values, accusations of incest can be used as a way to denigrate a particular group. For example, these jokes told in Georgia are used to put down other Southerners, including people from Alabama and Arkansas, mountain people, and "white trash":

Q: What does a teenage girl from Arkansas say before having sex?
A: Watch out Daddy, you're gonna crush my cigarettes.

Q: How do you castrate a redneck?
A: Hit his daughter on her chin.

Q: How do you know your sister has her period?
A: Your father's dick tastes like shit.

Q: How do you know if an Alabama girl is on her period?
A: Her brother's dick tastes funny.

There was this girl in a small town in Alabama who wanted to borrow the family truck one Saturday night. So she went to the den where her daddy was watching television and asked him for the keys. "Well, honey, if you really want to take it out tonight you can, but to get the keys you'll have to give me a blow job first." She agreed, and got down on her knees, unfastened his belt, unzipped his pants, pulled out his dick and started sucking. After a few minutes she stopped and said, "Ew, Daddy, this tastes like shit." "Yeah, I know," he told her, "Your brother needed my car for a date tonight."

A painful and destructive experience for women is reduced to jokes in which the girl cares more about her cigarettes than the incest or is willing to have sex in exchange for the car keys. Some of these jokes also suggest that both males and females can be targets. They give a clear message that the men of these groups are so low that incest is a common behavior (unlike the fraternity man who is so disturbed by his unintended—though criminal—incest) and that the women are so low that they don't even care.

Another aspect of these jokes is that in assigning incest stereotypically to the poorer classes of certain regions (the South and Appalachia in particular), the rest of the nation can maintain the fiction of moral superiority, and, within a region, one state or group can distance itself from the stereotype by pushing the accusations off on another. Anne Shelby (1999), writing about incest jokes as one form of "redneck" joke, points out that in small Appalachian communities, people pay careful attention to each other's histories and genealogies: "This information is important not just because it tells us who we are, though it does do that. It is also important because it guards against incest, which is strictly taboo. In a small community, you have to keep careful track" (p. 156).

Jokes, of course, can go a lot further than legends, in both the extremity of the action and in slurring a whole group—jokes, after all, are not supposed to be "true" whereas legends depend on at least the possibility of belief for their power (legends shade into jokes when the performer and audience refuse to grant even the possibility of credence). Jokes, however, with their reliance on shared expectations, can be just as powerful in reflecting and propagating a perceived reality.

The two sets of folklore discussed in this chapter—one involving men who "accidentally" commit or almost commit incest and a second involving "trash" who deliberately have sex with their own children of both sexes and don't even care—also represent a common and mistaken societal view: Good decent family men could not be guilty of such a crime, but there is certainly a "type" that could be guilty. Kondora (1997), exploring some of the popular media representation of cases of child sexual abuse, identified a theme "Embodiment of abuser: Monster vs model citizen" (p. 288). She quotes Wendy Kozol (1995, p. 657) in discussing the "monster" depiction which "ignores power relations and turns violence into something that only occurs in deranged families." The accused abusers who are presented as unlikely to be guilty are described as hard-working, church-going, family men. One of the quotations she refers to that best represents this viewpoint is from Pamela Freyd, executive director of the False Memory Syndrome Foundation (FMSF), who responded to the question of how the members of the organization know they are not representing pedophiles:

> We are a good looking bunch of people: graying hair, well-dressed, healthy, smiling . . . just about every person who has attended (FMSF Conference) is someone you would likely find interesting and want to count as a friend. (FMSF, 1992, p. 1, cited in Kondora, 1997, p. 294)

These descriptions and the folklore support each other in the view of the abuser as someone you would be able to pick out of a crowd in a small Southern town, for example, because they *look* the part. However, the businessmen or chatroom users or fraternity brothers are all seen as decent men ("well-dressed, healthy, smiling") who accidentally (almost) commit this act. It is an important goal for those who are committed to eliminating child sexual abuse to make sure people have the correct information—that people who sexually abuse children, whether related to them or not, are not limited to any particular group, by education, socioeconomic status, religion, race, geography, or any other demographic factor. Abusers of children, just like the abusers of adult women, often appear "normal" and are known as fine, upstanding citizens, often extremely friendly and likeable. The circulating folklore that perpetuates the false belief that only certain recognizable, degenerate types would be capable of deliberately abusing children, particularly their own daughters or sisters, makes it harder for survivors' stories to be accepted. It is difficult enough for most survivors of abuse to tell their stories, without the additional risk of being discredited because the alleged abuser was "well-dressed, healthy, smiling." By addressing these jokes about incest, an educator can both counter those stereotypes and give the message that child sexual abuse, whether inside or outside the family, is not a laughing matter.

9

THE STOLEN KIDNEY, LEAPING CRABS, AND OTHER DANGERS OF SEXUALITY

❏

Stolen Organs

I heard a story about nine or ten months ago about a man in Dallas, Texas who went out for a night on the town with a couple of friends. After several drinks he is aware of a beautiful girl watching him and following him. She approaches him, introduces herself, and explains that she is from out of town. He is very attracted to her, and she seems taken with him. Before long, the man tells his friends to go on without him, that he is going to see this beautiful woman home. The man returns to the woman's hotel room and they share another drink. She is really coming on at this point, and he likes it! The last thing the man remembers is sitting on the bed in the hotel room.

Then he awakens, feeling very groggy. He is now in bed, and tries to sit up, but his back is in excruciating pain. He reaches back and is bandaged around his lower back. Looking around, he realizes that he is not only in a different hotel room (in another hotel), but the beautiful girl is gone and it is two days *later. He immediately calls the front desk and has them call an ambulance and the police, realizing he has been assaulted in some way. He is taken to a nearby hospital and thoroughly examined. Upon returning, the doctor explained to the patient that he would be fine, but that his kidney had been professionally removed. The doctor explained that people have been robbed before for their vital organs, as they sell for several million dollars on the black market. This particular man was lucky though, as his life was spared; many aren't as lucky.*

If the "Welcome to the wonderful world of AIDS" legends have lost their impact in warning men against sex with strangers, these theft for transplant stories infuse fear of new dangers into one-night stands. In the past there have been numerous stories of men being robbed after sex, often having been drugged, but being robbed of an organ brings these stories up-to-date. As in the previous version, other versions emphasize the danger of a man straying from his buddies:

It supposedly happened to my friend's T.A.'s friend. A group of friends went to Atlanta for the weekend. They decided to go out to one of the clubs for dancing and drinking. One of the guys told his friends he was leaving for a couple of hours and he would meet them back at the club. A few hours went by and he didn't return to the club. The friends decided he would probably just meet them at the hotel, so they left. When they woke up he hadn't returned and they started to get worried. About noon they got a call from their friend at the hospital. They went to pick him up and he told them a horrifying story. He thought he was going to the girl's apartment. Before they got there, he got really tired. When he woke up he was in an empty warehouse alone. He moved to get up and felt a sharp pain shoot through his lower back. He felt the place where the pain came from and there was a huge cut there. He found his way out and took a taxi to the hospital. During the night he had been drugged and his kidney had been removed. Apparently there is an underground market for vital organs. He was just the latest victim.

This story has made its way through oral tellings and the Internet in a number of forms, often with information or commentary that may convince readers that it is a true story. Some versions report that a friend or relative is a paramedic in a particular city in which this activity has occurred and that the paramedics have all received training in treating victims of these organ thefts, as in the following example of commentary that accompanied a recounting of the story found on a listserver:

> This is not a scam or out of a science fiction novel, it is real. It is documented and confirmable. If you travel or someone close to you travels, please be careful. Sadly, this is very true. My husband is a Houston Firefighter/EMT and they have received alerts regarding this crime ring. It is to be taken very seriously. The daughter of a friend of a fellow firefighter had this happen to her. Skilled doctor's [sic] are performing these crimes! (which, by the way have been highly noted in the Las Vegas area). Additionally, the military has received alerts regarding this. This story blew me away. I really want as many people to see this as possible so please bounce this to whoever you can.

A number of people have reported that it has been sent to them at work as a warning about travel dangers in general or in specific cities, Las Vegas being one commonly mentioned. The image of Las Vegas as dominated by drink, drugs, sex, gambling, and organized crime provides a believable locale. Even though some of those forwarding it have indicated that they are unsure of the veracity of the story, they still feel an obligation to pass on the warning just in case. This story frequently stimulates discussions about whether it really could have happened. Some suggest that no one would go through the trouble of the careful surgery, removal of only one kidney, paying for a motel room and leaving warnings to prevent the victim from dying, as described in some variants, such as the one below; they say anyone who would do something like this would just take both kidneys and leave the victims to die in a back alley.

Some of the versions do not involve a pick-up by a beautiful woman but simply a drugged drink; these tellings change the warnings from the dangers of women and sexuality to the dangers of drinking in an unfamiliar situation or accepting drinks from strangers. However, the woman as a seducer who then drugs the man is much more prevalent in these stories and, even when the warning seems to be about drinking, the woman seducer is often present:

> My mother told me to be careful when going out to bars. She said that she had a friend of hers that knew somebody who went drinking one night in a bar. After drinking, he went back to this woman's apartment, where he blacked out, and didn't wake up until the next morning. He was laying in a bathtub covered in ice, with a phone next to him and the words "DIAL 911 OR YOU WILL DIE" written on the medicine cabinet. He called 911, and found out that he had been operated on, and his kidney had been stolen for the black market. The police told him not to move, and that if he got up out of the bathtub, he would die.
>
> My mother told me this over the phone one night, telling me to be careful if I were to go drinking in any bars. She said to me to be careful who you went drinking with, or who buys you drinks, because that person might slip something into it.

Even though the mother clearly tells her son that this story is a warning about the danger that lies in drinking in bars or with the wrong people, the story does involve a woman who takes the victim back to her apartment. It may be that many mothers are uncomfortable talking to their sons about sex and pick-ups in bars. By telling this story, they can overtly focus on the drinking issue, while still including the warning about sex. Goska (1997) specifically addresses what these stories reflect about how some men view women:

> Circulation of legends of theft of male organs by females serves to create a narrative reality. In this reality, women prey on men, not men on women; women enter and violate men's bodies; and women get something, both a material and a metaphorical something, from the sexual encounter, while men are lessened, both physically and emotionally "used." (P. 208)

Goska expands this argument and describes the view that what happens to the men in these stories is very similar to rape. The drug that knocks them out is also similar to Rohypnol, the "rape drug," since it is not detected by the man in his drink and induces amnesia after a certain point in the evening's activities. Most warnings about Rohypnol on college campuses are targeted at women and emphasize ways to prevent someone from spiking their drinks with it. The kidney theft stories more often focus on the danger from the woman, not on the danger of a drugged drink. It is interesting that we have only rarely heard versions of the stolen kidney story that involve a woman as the victim, but in the examples we do have, the emphasis is on the danger of drugged drinks. While the male victim version may deal with metaphorical rape or even castration anxiety, there is no need for legends that present women as victims of *metaphorical* rape for the simple reason that women face the much more likely danger of *real* rape. It also may be that, as with the "Welcome to the wonderful world of AIDS" stories, the bar pickup scenario does not work for women. If the stolen kidney story appears with a woman as unintentional organ donor, the narrative would more likely have to be based on romance and courtship. It is easy to envision stories of courtship of a woman on holiday in an "exotic" location that end with amateur surgery rather than a gift-wrapped coffin.

Though kidney theft has not been documented as a real danger, the warnings in this story may be useful in other ways. On many campuses, for example, drinking for the sake of becoming drunk is a major form of recreation. The reminder that drinking either by itself or with other drugs (intentionally used by the drinker for a quick, cheap "drunk," or inflicted by someone else slipping it in) can lead to a state in which the person is extremely vulnerable to sexual assault and to robbery, even if not to kidney surgery, is a useful one, which can be extricated during discussion of this story. Another dimension of fear for women was added to the warnings about Rohypnol in a message, circulated on the Internet in 2000, which begins, "Ladies, be more alert and cautious when getting a drink offer from a guy." It proceeds to describe a (nonexistent) drug called Progesterex, which allegedly can be dissolved in a drink as unnoticeably as Rohypnol and causes instant and permanent sterility. The rumor is that rapists use it at the same time as Rohypnol so that pregnancy cannot occur and paternity cannot be traced to them. While it seems the fear of Rohypnol, which is real, would be enough to cause caution, perhaps warnings about Rohypnol have become commonplace, part of the background noise of contemporary fears, so that the extra warning about a new, though nonexistent, danger serves the effect of a booster shot for cautious behavior. Moreover, the horror of permanent sterility, of harm to the female reproductive system, coupled with rape combines two of the most serious threats in legends directed at women.

Revenge of the Spurned Woman

There was this big church wedding. The minister got to the part when he asks if anybody has any reason why the couple shouldn't get married. And the bride says in a loud voice, "I do. My fiancé slept with one of my bridesmaids last night after the rehearsal dinner!"

This legend illustrates another danger from women to men appearing in folklore and popular culture—the actions of vengeful women who have been cheated on or rejected. In the story above, the action is public humiliation of the groom, but there are also more violent stories. In one of the many shocking scenes in the film *Fatal Attraction,* the rejected woman, seeking revenge after a brief affair ends, kills the pet rabbit of her ex-lover's family. This theme of punishing men by killing their pets also appears in these contemporary legends collected in Georgia:

In A . . . a girl hung her boyfriend's dog because she caught him in bed with another girl.

In T . . . , Georgia at L . . . High School, a girl hung her boyfriend's dog when she found out he was seeing another girl.

At D . . . High School in D . . . a girl had a friend hang her boyfriend's dog off his front porch when she caught him with another girl.

The man who collected these also adds that he has heard versions in which the young woman poisons or shoots her ex-boyfriend's dog. The viciousness of the revenge reinforces the belief that "hell hath no fury like a woman scorned" but implies that women are too weak (or cowardly) to take direct revenge against the objects of their anger. While these legends may be heard by some as warnings against cheating on a girlfriend, they are also very easy to read as examples of the view that women can be very dangerous, especially when driven by jealousy or anger at rejection. It is also interesting to note that these stories represent the reverse of the usual pattern seen in violent relationships as reported by workers in the area of domestic violence: In general, if women are violent in a relationship, the violence ends when the relationship ends; if men are violent, the violence escalates when the relationship ends. It would also be interesting to know if these legends are more common in rural and suburban areas where young men are more likely to have pet dogs. There are numerous examples in fiction and the popular media of women destroying prized objects belonging to cheating partners and ex-husbands. Expensive cars figure predominantly in these, as in the scene in the film *Waiting to Exhale* in which an angry deserted wife puts all her (soon-to-be) ex-husband's clothes and possessions in his car and sets the car on fire. While many may enjoy vicariously the destruction of an expensive car as a form of revenge, the killing of pets will probably make the victim/avenger much less sympathetic while the cheating boyfriend will garner much more support.

It would be interesting to use these stories as the starting point for a class discussion about the appropriate actions and reactions if a boyfriend or girlfriend cheats. In the same way that education needs to focus on identifying the components of healthy relationships, it is important to identify healthy responses and communication in stressful situations, as well as defining healthy ways to end relationships.

Jokes about Battering

Whereas the stories above focus on the terrible revenge a woman might have on a man through killing his pet, most of the folklore about men battering women is in the form of jokes. It is important to remember that jokes serve as a socially sanctioned outlet for taboo ideas and subjects. They can be seen as a way to say what someone really thinks without taking the responsibility of stating his or her opinion. If someone is angered or put off by the joke, the teller can remind the listener that "it's only a joke." Because of this layer of protection the joke provides, jokes often give a very clear view into a group's attitudes and concerns. Jokes can also serve the function of reinforcing a community's or group's values, increasing group cohesion and excluding outsiders. By making it clear what is considered funny and who is the appropriate object or target of a group's humor, the joketellers can bring group members into line on how they should feel about certain people or topics. These jokes about battered women serve to undermine the years of work of the battered women's movement in trying to educate the police, the legal system, the health care system, social services, and the general population, about the seriousness and extent of battering:

Q: What do all battered women have in common?
A: (Slapping hand in rhythm with words) They don't fucking listen!

Q: What do you tell a woman with two black eyes?
A: Nothing. You already told her twice.

Q: What do you do if your dishwasher stops working?
A: Slap her.

Q: How many battered women does it take to screw in a light bulb?
A: Just one if she knows what's good for her.

Q: What is the first thing a woman does after leaving the battered women's shelter?
A: The dishes, if she knows what's good for her.

Q: What's worse than a male chauvinist pig?
A: A woman who won't do what she's told.

These jokes can be read in a number of ways. That is, they can be seen as a statement about how some men feel women should be treated, with these jokes presenting a view of the naturalness of using violence to punish women who don't "know what's good for them." They may be read as a way of reinforcing the view that battering is not serious and can be laughed at, that battered women are appropriate targets of humor, and that batterers are not criminals. The jokes may also serve as a form of indirect aggression against feminists who have tried to change the views of battering expressed in these jokes. Or they may also possibly be seen as a critique of the views of such men, that is, the attitudes expressed here are being mocked since they may be seen as such obvious exaggerations. For example, slapping a woman who stops washing the dishes may be seen as outrageous behavior and, therefore, the man who does it is the butt of the humor. However, battered women, formerly battered women, and those who work with them all would say the attitudes expressed in these jokes are not exaggerations but accurate statements of the views of many batterers. Certainly, the public is much more aware of domestic violence after years of work on public education by the domestic violence movement and publicity through celebrity examples, such as the O. J. Simpson case. However, the hope that discussion of these issues would create more sensitivity has obviously not been realized. These jokes can then also be read as a backlash against the gains of the battered women's movement, masking hostility with humor.

If jokes such as these come up in a discussion, they can be handled in a straightforward way by asking the same kinds of questions we've asked about them. What makes jokes like these "funny" is the unexpectedness of the answer, but it's useful to push beyond that in a discussion to ask who are we laughing at and why. Is it funny that a man would slap a woman for not doing the dishes or would "tell" her something by punching her in the eye? A group discussion can then move into the issue of whether it is ever appropriate to use physical force in a relationship, what we know about the prevalence and consequences of violence in relationships, and what can be done to change attitudes. By the end of the conversation, we can hope that we would have "ruined a good joke," as anyone who questions the message that a joke conveys is often told, so that domestic violence never is a laughing matter for these students.

Painful Piercing

In the first chapter, we noted that as folklore keeps up with changing fashions, there are legends beginning to circulate about body piercing.

This story was collected by a college man from a woman about a high school friend:

> This young woman turned eighteen and had her clitoris pierced as soon as she could afford it. She wanted to have that pierced because she didn't know anyone who had had theirs pierced. A couple of weeks later, she began dating a fellow and urged him to have his penis pierced with a Prince Albert (a barbell through the head of the penis). He finally agreed and had it done. They didn't have sex for some time after that, for he was swollen and sore. When the pain of the piercing finally subsided they decide to have sex. As they were having sex, though, the phone rang and he pulled himself out of her. In doing this, unfortunately, his Prince Albert caught her clitoral ring and pulled it out, tearing much of her clitoris with it. She was forced to go to the hospital, though she was stable. She broke up with him a week later and has not had sex with anyone since. I have no information about the fellow.

The student who collected this said it might be used as a warning to "discourage genital piercings, or perhaps even to discourage sex itself." Since many unpierced people often wonder about the safety and potential discomforts of lip, nose, and tongue piercings, particularly of rings getting caught (dangers of nose-blowing?), this kind of story would easily gain wide circulation. Such stories may also be thought of as the up-to-date versions of adolescents getting their braces locked together when kissing. However, the young people in this story are punished both for piercing their genitals and for their sexual activity, whereas in the earlier stories adolescents are punished for sexual experimentation but not for orthodonture. As usual, the woman is punished more than the man, perhaps additionally so because she is the one who convinced him to have his penis pierced; her clitoris is torn but nothing apparently happens to him except that they break up. The story of her serious injury confirms the worst fears of people uncomfortable with piercing, allows people to discuss a sensitive anxiety-producing topic, and provides a handy warning against piercing.

For individuals who have been pierced or are seriously considering it, the warnings may be taken as simply to exercise care so that injury doesn't occur, rather than a warning against piercing. Given the prevalence of piercing of many body parts, it should be discussed as a health issue at least at the high school and college levels. There are risks of infection, which can be prevented by careful checking of the procedures used before going ahead and by following directions for care of the piercing afterward. For particularly sensitive body parts, it is important to find out answers to questions such as whether nipple piercing could affect breast-feeding or whether clitoral or penile piercing could affect the sexual response. In a university women's health class, an initial discussion section on reproductive and sexual anatomy was redirected by students into a discussion of clitoral piercing, so the interest is clearly there. A health educator could present piercing the way any health-related decision would be approached, in terms of risks and benefits and personal values. The issue of needle sterilization can be connected to discussion of blood-borne infectious diseases such as HIV and hepatitis C, while at the same time there could be a discussion of why people want to have body parts pierced. We haven't yet heard any stories about tattooing, which is another activity about which adults, especially parents of adolescents, would probably appreciate having warning stories.

Leaping Crabs and Other Sexually Transmitted Diseases

While AIDS is currently the sexually transmitted disease most feared, other diseases still have a place in folklore. Surprisingly, even in 2000 there are a number of stories about crabs, also known as pubic lice:

A girl I knew from high school had become an exotic dancer at an upscale club in Atlanta. I was talking to her about other clubs and she described one as a "jack shack," . . . a low-class establishment where men could openly masturbate, and prostitution occurred.

She then told me a story about a man, unfamiliar with the club's reputation, who went there one night after work. He found a girl in particular that he liked, and she performed several table and lap dances for him, completely nude.

Several days later, the man was having problems with one of his eyes. He went to see his opthamologist to have it checked out, suspecting an infection like pink eye. After examining the man, the doctor asked him what he had been doing lately. The man said nothing and asked why. The doctor replied, "I just extracted a pubic louse from your eye." So apparently a crab had jumped from the stripper's pubic hair into his eye.

A girl we knew was watching a male stripper at Mardi Gras when a crab jumped off his crotch and flew into her eye.

Told to me when I was around 14–15, by an older friend. She was 18 I believe, and she told me this story using her friend as a basis. The [name of club] is a male strip club in Atlanta. The girl was there for her eighteenth birthday, and was treated to a lap dance by a male stripper. When he was doing pelvic thrusts, a crab, an STD, flew from his crotch into her eye. A week later her eye was inflamed and needed medical attention. Her mother found out she had visited the club, grounded her, and filed a lawsuit against the club.

My old roommate told me she had a friend that went to a bachelorette party at [Name] Club and they watched the male strippers. I have never been to that establishment but I have heard that they have both male and female dancers that perform totally nude. During the performance one of the girls supposedly got something in her eye. Well, her eye irritated her all night, she went home and couldn't sleep because the irritation just got worse and worse. The next day the girl went to the doctor where they removed a crab lice from her eye.

The first time I heard this I believed it. I was disgusted and thought to myself I would never go to a strip club again (or if I did at least wear some Chemistry lab goggles), but I heard the story from another friend of mine. This version was about a gay friend of hers who went to an all male-strip club in New Orleans and the same thing occurred to this guy. When she told me this story, my reaction was "oh, that's just a bunch of bull" and I told her about hearing my version of the story. We both had a good laugh because we both believed such a silly story.

No matter how unlikely these stories are, they are certainly popular. Crabs are crab-like lice "that live in pubic hair and occasionally in the hair of the chest, armpits, eyelashes, and eyebrows and are usually transmitted by intimate physical contact" (Boston Women's Health Book Collective, 1998, pp. 634–35). They can also travel from one body to cloth, such as towels and bedding, and then onto another person. They cannot leap long distances from person to person and they need a hairy environment—not an eye—to survive. It might be possible that if someone had his or her face in the pubic hair of another person, a louse could crawl into the eyebrows and live there, but would not take up residence in the eye. If these stories are so improbable, why do they persist? In general, an infestation of crabs is very uncomfortable, with severe itching, but it is curable. The main issue seems to be that it is embarrassing, both because some people incorrectly associate it with a lack of cleanliness and also because it is a sign that someone has probably been sexually active. Much of the folklore discussed in this book, from the sperm cells on the microscope slide to the surprise party, are about the revelation to others—classmates, co-workers, teachers—of an individual's sexual practices. In these stories of strippers and pubic lice, the victim has merely been watching, though the emphasis on the eye makes clear that even watching is societally unacceptable. The doctor who discovers the lice in the eye (and whoever else then finds out) may believe that there was intimate sexual contact and the explanation that it happened at a strip joint makes it just as embarrassing as if there had been sexual contact.

Another view of the stories about crabs is that these serve to provide a concrete and understandable illustration of transmission of STDs. Bacteria and viruses are not visible to the naked eye and viruses cannot be seen under a light microscope, as bacteria can, but require an electron microscope. There is a great deal of anxiety about how invisible "germs" are transmitted, as can be seen in the number of advertisements that feature germs, made visible through animation, lurking in bathrooms, kitchens, and other breeding areas. Antibacterial soaps and antibacterial "waterless" soaps are popular items. Lice, though not easy to see, are visible. It is reasonable, though inaccurate, to imagine an insect leaping from pubic hair as a means of transmission. These stories may help to make concrete the anxieties about transmission. Unfortunately, the belief about lice transmission, as expressed in these legends, is a poor model for other disease transmission and may ultimately serve to confuse the listeners. If, for example, people believe that AIDS is caused by a virus that can leap off a dancer's genitals and infect an onlooker, they will not be concentrating on real risks but may suffer from unjustified anxieties. Unfortunately, even when people know the "scientific facts," that does not prevent anxiety. Using these stories in a class can lead from a discussion of how crabs are really transmitted and how they are treated to broader issues of transmission of other kinds of STDs, with an opportunity to clarify the areas of danger and safety that exist.

Other diseases that may be transmitted sexually also continue to appear in folklore:

This guy was at a party, and when he went to leave the hostess gave him a huge kiss. He noticed after the kiss that the hostess had a big nasty cold sore on her lip. He didn't think anything of

it. Later, he was with his girlfriend and gave her oral sex. He ended up giving her herpes, too.

A girl at college had this cold sore on her face and washed it and then left the washcloth sitting in the sink. Her roommate gets her period unexpectedly, comes back, and cleans herself off with the same washcloth. The second girl contracts herpes in the same way.

This guy has oral sex with a girl who's menstruating. He notices white spots in his mouth. He's gotten thrush from her yeast infection.

Today at work I was going to eat shrimp fried rice from the Chinese restaurant in the mall, but a story that my assistant manager told me changed my mind. She said that one of the girls in her cosmetology class said one of her friends got sick from eating at one of the local Chinese restaurants. The girl thought she had food poisoning. She went to the doctor and he told her it wasn't food poisoning, but syphilis. She said that she didn't get sick until after she ate the shrimp fried rice at the Chinese restaurant. The doctor asked if she had any left over. She did, so she brought it in and the doctor tested it. Four samples of semen were found in the rice and one was carrying syphilis.

The first and third stories focus on an important issue in transmission of some STDs, which is that diseases can be transmitted between the genitals and the mouth. Cold sores on the mouth and lips are caused by herpes simplex virus Type I (HSV I), while genital herpes is usually caused by Type II (HSV II). However, sexuality and health educators are usually quick to point out, as *Our Bodies, Ourselves* (Boston Women's Health Book Collective, 1998) does, that "while HSV I is usually found above the waist and HSV II below, there is some crossover, primarily caused by the increasing practice of oral-genital sex" (p. 351). Yeast infections, caused by a fungus, can also be transmitted between mouth and genitals (in either direction). Pre-AIDS, very few people who were not health professionals were probably aware of the possibility of oral thrush, as a yeast infection of the mouth is called. Both oral and genital yeast infections can flourish when the immune system is not functioning well. One of the early identified HIV-associated opportunistic infections was oral thrush, though it took a long time before persistent, recurring vaginal yeast infections were also recognized as a possible sign that a woman was HIV positive. In this story, the fact that the woman was menstruating also is significant, as women are more likely to experience yeast infections around the time they menstruate. These stories provide a useful warning that infections can be transmitted orally, so that, in terms of disease transmission, oral sex cannot be thought of as a "safe" alternative to vaginal or anal intercourse. The first story also presents the correct information that kissing someone with a cold sore can transmit the virus. Even though it is less likely that the man could have passed on the virus to his girlfriend when he had no symptoms, it is certainly possible. The second story raises the issue of transmission of herpes through an inanimate object. The virus can survive on a damp washcloth for at least a short period of time, so this story is also possible; it would depend on the length of time between when each of two roommates used the washcloth. A wet washcloth could also transmit other diseases, such as the infection of the vagina caused by a protozoan called trichomonas. Shared sex toys can also transmit herpes and other diseases.

While the first three stories, whether they happened or not, do convey some useful warnings, the last story is in another category. There is nothing in the story that is plausible. Syphilis cannot be transmitted through food; it requires very direct sexual contact. The first sign or symptom of syphilis would not be confused with food poisoning: A hard painless ulcer called a chancre appears near the site of contact, anywhere from about a week to three months after exposure. Having demonstrated the impossibility of the story, there are other interesting aspects of the legend. In the chapter on menstruation, we raised the theme of tampering with food, which appears in recurring stories about cooks and other food handlers who contribute their own bodily fluids to food. There are a number of stories about men ejaculating into food, particularly involving disgruntled employees of fast food chains (see, for example, Langlois, 1991). This theme is combined with a recurring racist theme that targets Chinese restaurants as sites of bizarre culinary practices. There are legends in many cities about health inspectors closing down a Chinese restaurant after finding cats in the freezer. One student collected a story that combined two sets of legends: A woman got ill after eating a chicken dish at a Chinese restaurant. The doctor checked the "chicken"; it turned out to be a cat with VD. This story has removed any possible sexual element (ejaculate) from the transmission and ignores that fact that cooking would destroy most STDs. After all, these organisms are transmitted sexually because they cannot live outside the body for a long time and must be transmitted by close contact, usually between bodily fluid and mucus membrane. Another variant combines the elements of xenophobia, food taboos, and disease with a slightly different twist:

> A woman became very ill and went to the doctor. When they tested the Chinese food she had left over in her refrigerator, it turned out that it was made from the uterus of a cat with a yeast infection.

The professor who reported he had heard this story in his class said that the women seemed much more grossed out than the men—perhaps because only the women could appreciate the significance of a yeast infection. Besides fast food restaurants (Kentucky Fried rats and equally disgusting stories about other chains), legends seem to target few ethnic restaurants other than Chinese. One story focuses on Korean restaurants serving dog meat. However, it is likely that in particular locations, where other ethnic groups have established popular restaurants, similar stories may surface. This story, which clearly implies that four separate men masturbated into the food, is similar to the story of the fraternity ritual which involved masturbating on a pizza; however, in this story the unknowing customer is the one to eat it.

Embarrassing Sexual Adventures

There are a number of other legends that focus less on the terrifying and more on the unpleasant and embarrassing. Some of the embarrassment stories, as with the sperm on the slide and the crabs stories, have to do with the sexual activity of an individual being accidentally revealed. For example, one story circulated about a girl in junior high who had pubic hairs stuck in her braces (in some cases the same girl who masturbated with a hot dog, who has obviously moved on to fellatio with hot dog substitutes). Other stories focus on bodily functions out of control in sexual situations, which may reflect some of the anxieties related to a lack of knowledge about sexual function. For example, a lot of younger boys are worried that they will urinate during sexual activity, not realizing that there is physiological protection against mixing ejaculation and urination. As they get older, this is usually less of a worry, but the idea of orgasm as a loss of control combined with discomfort about oral sex triggers other sorts of stories:

> This story was told to me by my roommate in boarding school my senior year. There were two guys and they bet each other that they could have sex with more people than the other, but the catch was that Jim had to watch Joe—vice-versa—when they were having sex. Jim picks up Jane and he calls Joe to tell him that he is coming home and to hide in the closet so that he can witness the event. Jane was having stomach problems all day long and had even had a bad case of diarrhea. Jane and Jim started fooling around and one thing led to another and they started having sex. Throughout the process Jane's stomach started feeling upset. She was getting worked up to an orgasm

and as she came she exploded. Her excrement was all over Jim, and Joe came laughing out of the closet. Jane grabbed her clothes and ran out.

The story contains the male spectatorship issues described previously. If Joe's presence had been known to Jane, without her having diarrhea, she probably would have run out of the room after grabbing her clothes. However, this story adds to the humiliation of being observed having sex with that of having lost control of her bowels. Jim, instead of being one-up on Joe in the competition, is embarrassed by being covered in excrement.

Vomiting stories are very common. The stories don't always clarify what causes the vomiting, that is, whether her stomach is already upset, whether she has a really strong gag reflex, whether he is not particularly clean, etc.:

I was reminded recently of high school lore centering around the presence of vomit in embarrassing situations. The two of these I found most popular was the girl that threw up while kissing the guy, and the girl who was performing orally on a guy and vomits on his penis. Interestingly enough, both of these tales have *the girl* who is creating a gross and embarrassing situation.

I heard this story from my friend, this is firsthand information. He was in a van leaving a concert and this girl was sucking him and she threw up all over his stomach because he gagged her with his thingy.

Oral sex has appeared in various forms in the folklore in this book: women using peanut butter to induce a dog and tuna fish to seduce a man to perform oral sex, both resulting in awful consequences for the woman. Cunnilingus is presented as very unappealing but something women want to experience. Conversely, fellatio is also presented as something that men want but women may not enjoy—to the point of vomiting. Other folklore reinforces the desire men have for fellatio and women's reluctance to perform it. For example, one of a series of negative jokes about married women refers to this:

Q: What's the difference between your wife and your job?
A: After 5 years your job will still suck.

Besides the risk of vomiting, there are also stories that present other dangers from oral sex, particularly in cars:

I heard about this guy that was getting head from this girl and when he came he flipped his truck because he lost control. I actually know this guy, but have not heard the story from his mouth.

On the same subject, I also heard about a guy in the same situation, but instead of flipping, he got pulled over for speeding and said that his girlfriend was sick.

Obviously, the pleasure of fellatio is so intense for these men and causes such a loss of control that one flips the car and another is arrested for speeding. During a famous literary blowjob, in *The World According to Garp,* a man's penis was bitten off when his parked car was rammed, emphasizing another potential danger. In this case it is not the folkloric toothed vagina that presents dangers to a man's penis, but the toothed mouth.

According to folklore, oral sex provides an interesting heterosexual dilemma: Both men and women want to be the recipients and neither wants to be the performer. The general, though not necessarily correct, assumption is that gay men and lesbians by definition enjoy performing oral sex, thus the derogatory terms "cocksucker" and "muff diver."

Oral sex became a much more open topic of discussion in the wake of media reports involving President Clinton's sexual activity. Many discussions and jokes focused on the president's careful definition of a sexual relationship that did not include oral sex performed on him. In many ways, this is a logical outcome of the intercourse-centered definition of sex. "Going all the way" and "doing it" are very specifically terms meaning having vaginal-penile intercourse, not meaning, for example, reaching orgasm in various ways. Therefore, a woman who has experienced anal intercourse and cunnilingus and has performed fellatio may still see herself as a virgin, having not been "sexually active" by her own definition, that used by the general public and even some sexuality researchers. Clinton's response, which has been described as technical hairsplitting, is not any more hairsplitting than the common kind of writing that talks about teenage sexual activity as if the only activity that counts is intercourse. At the same time as the impeachment hearings, an article published in the *Journal of the American Medical Association* (Sanders and Reinisch, 1999) reported that of a large number of college students surveyed, 59 percent believed oral-genital contact did not constitute "having sex." It is not surprising that if the experts on sexuality often use the term sexual activity to mean intercourse, then the rest of the world is entitled to say they haven't had a sexual relationship if there has been no penetration. One of the issues this points to is that health and sexuality educators and researchers need to be a lot more careful about how they use terms. For example, to say that a goal is for more sexually active teenagers to use condoms does not acknowledge the fact that some of that activity might not require a condom. It would make more sense to be very specific about naming vaginal intercourse if that's what we mean, but to keep a broad spectrum of sexual behaviors under the category of sexual activity.

When using folklore in the classroom, it is impossible to predict with any assurance what kinds of stories may surface. For example, in many years of collecting, there had been none on jumping crabs and then suddenly there were a number in one year; for awhile the only stories of sexually transmitted diseases focused on AIDS and then other STDs reappeared in the folklore. There are always new twists on old stories. The tanning bed story with which we began this book has recently evolved variants in which the young woman, instead of cooking her insides, catches crabs or herpes. New legendry similarly identifies strip joints as dangerous due not only to leaping crabs, but also, in another legend, to flying sweat carrying a herpes infection into the viewer's eye. This chapter on dangers gives a sense of the variety of issues that may surface, some of which seem funny but many of which are extremely painful, sensitive topics. Even though an unexpected piece of folklore may completely reshape the direction of the planned learning experience, it also is an assurance that the material is changing to adjust to the interests, anxieties, fears, and concerns of the learners.

10

I DON'T BELIEVE THIS BUT MY FRIENDS DO

Using Folklore in Sexuality Education

❑

The Current State of Sexuality Education

Sexuality education is one of the most controversial areas of the school curriculum. The debates about abstinence-only curricula versus more comprehensive curricula are as intense as those between anti-abortion and pro-choice groups. Researchers have consistently shown that abstinence-only education (that is, where abstinence is presented as the *only* possible option for teenagers, or even adults who are not married, and there is no education about contraception or safer sex) does not work in reducing teenage sexual activity or pregnancy. On the other hand, research has found some degree of success (using such measures as delay in first intercourse, use of contraceptives, numbers of partners) with abstinence-plus programs, which emphasize abstinence but also discuss contraceptives and prevention of STD transmission (Kirby, 1997). However, the U.S. Congress undermined researchers and educators by earmarking $88 million in federal and matching state funds to be used for abstinence-*only* education. That means, for example, these funds could not be used in educational programs in which abstinence is promoted as the best option, but in which students also learn about condom use. Abstinence-only approaches often rely heavily on fear tactics. If contraception or safer sex is discussed at all, it is to teach that they don't work—using incorrect statistics about condom breakage and exaggerated claims about dangerous side-effects of other contraceptives. Sexual violence is often used as a warning to young women not to start any sexual activity (even kissing) because it leads to uncontrollable arousal of the male, who then may commit sexual assault. In these curricula, nothing seems very positive about sexuality until it is transformed by monogamous marriage into something safe and wonderful.

Although many states require sexuality education, they have very different regulations about what can and cannot be presented in the curriculum. Some require a comprehensive curriculum, while others specifically prohibit discussion of such topics as abortion or homosexuality. Many school districts and individual administrators or teachers avoid controversial topics because they are worried about repercussions from what is often a small vocal minority in a community. A few documented horror stories (not legends), such as a teacher who was fired after bringing in a gay speaker to a classroom, serve to keep the curriculum on "safe" ground. Surveys of students indicate that they are often most interested in learning about the very topics that are not being addressed. They want to know about contraception, abortion, homosexuality, masturbation, and they are certainly talking about those topics, as the folklore in this book clearly indicates. The idea that young people can be protected by keeping certain topics out of the classroom is as absurd as the approach in which it is assumed that if you don't talk about drugs in class, no adolescent will ever think of trying them. Students are talking to each other about a wide range of topics related to sexuality, without any impetus from the curriculum, but the information transmitted through their conversation—including legends, beliefs, and jokes— often contains misinformation, not just about scientific "facts" but also in terms of the stereotyping of populations, whether it is gay men or "rednecks." Educators need to intervene in these conversations and facilitate learning that would draw on shared beliefs and understandings of the students. While there are many people who may be horrified at the suggestion that many topics in this book should be discussed in classrooms, would they be any less horrified to know these conversations are going on in the hallways and locker rooms? Folklore provides one opportunity for these discussions to be moved into an environment in which appropriate information can be provided and in which there can be a discussion about values, ethics, and such topics as discrimination and violence.

Multicultural Sexuality Education

A search for literature that looks at multicultural sexuality education is very frustrating. If anything does come up, it usually involves a juxtaposition of those words in ways that do not focus on teaching sexuality education from a multicultural perspective. James T. Sears, the author of one of the few articles on the topic, points out:

> Sex and love, menarche and menopause, incest and prostitution, condoms and diaphragms, marriage and dating, homosexuality and bisexuality, abstinence and promiscuity, masturbation and contraception, AIDS and STDs: although the descriptions of these terms are straightforward, their meanings are not. How adolescents and educators make sense of these concepts and how they understand their emerging sexual selves often vary according to the culture. These are reflected in observable differences such as the age of first intercourse, the meaning of rape, the incidence of AIDS, and attitudes toward sex education. . . . Those who have examined issues of culture and the teaching of sexuality conclude that conventional

sexuality education ignores multicultural populations . . . ;
multicultural sexuality education programmes are practically
non-existent. (Sears, 1997, p. 273)

Even adults from the same culture may be wrong about the ways adolescents "make sense of these concepts," for although they may share
certain aspects of a culture and may think they remember what it is like
being young, each generation has a different cultural context. Think
about the differences for the first generation of young women who had
access to oral contraceptives compared to their mothers' experiences related to pregnancy prevention, or the difference between the pre-AIDS
Woodstock generation and today's adolescents in terms of their views on
the dangers of STDs. Sexuality educators must always consider how to
reach students across such differences as age, race/ethnicity, religion,
gender, sexual orientation, and class. Some educators see sexuality as an
immutable given of physiology, thereby presenting it as a science topic,
and many still inappropriately see science as objective and neutral and,
therefore, not subject to culture. Fortunately, just as there are some science educators who have identified the need and the possibility for multicultural science education, there are now some sexuality educators
who see their subject the same way.

Folklore's Role in Multicultural Sexuality Education

There are a number of definitions and understandings of the term multicultural education. For the purpose of this discussion, we will focus on
the definition provided by James A. Banks (1997): "Multicultural education is also an educational reform movement that tries to reform
schools in ways that will give all students an equal opportunity to learn.
It describes teaching strategies that empower all students and give them
voice" (p. 68). Attempts at multicultural education in a variety of topics often fail because of the artificial nature of the attempts to bring

multicultural material into the classroom. Educators may spend a lot of time looking for the right books, posters, music, and, proudly presenting it, find that members of the ethnic group involved do not relate to the material. With folklore, class composition and the composition of the students' communities determine what is presented and discussed. When the approach is that all people use and create folklore, that it is not something limited to the international students in your class or a small specific subculture, then the show-and-tell exoticizing that may accompany less successful attempts at multicultural education will be prevented. The class will not suffer from what has been termed the "saris and samosas" approach, that is identifying a few cultural elements, such as dress and food of a particular culture, as a substitute for a deeper understanding of the culture. When the students provide the folklore, the teacher does not impose his or her own cultural expectations. In addition, the issues of power and resistance that need to be part of multicultural education are usually easy to elicit from folklore.

Educators often turn to popular culture to stimulate discussions of particular topics. For example, music videos provide an excellent opening to discuss issues of sexuality and violence. However, a drawback of using popular culture is that much of it is produced *for* a particular group but not *by* it, and, also, it becomes out of date quickly. Unless the students bring in their own material, an instructor runs the risk of presenting material that no longer speaks to the students or that, in fact, never did. Even if selected appropriately for one group of students, another group, perhaps Hmong or Latino students or sorority members or jocks or Goths, may tune out. Using folklore doesn't run the same risks, because, of course, students bring it in themselves; it is what they are hearing and spreading and, quite often, believing and acting on. As they repeat the folklore, they are also modifying it, adding their own personal stamp and, thereby, gaining ownership. It is important for educators to pay attention to the popular culture that their students enjoy, whether it is magazines, comics, videos, video games, television. This is not for the purpose of appearing hip, cool, or whatever is the appropriate term of the moment, to their students. It is to see what is engaging them and what can be learned about concerns and anxieties. Folklore can serve the same purpose.

While some folklore may appear frivolous and merely entertaining, much of it reflects very real concerns and anxieties. Legends about AIDS contracted from romantic strangers and gang-rape at a fraternity speak to shared fears about STD and HIV transmission and the prevalence of sexual violence. Even though relatively few people actually worry about having a kidney stolen for a transplant, that legend also can be mined for deeper fears and anxieties. By beginning with the folklore, these issues can be explored as they arise during discussion. Students are generally very good at analyzing the material once they have been encouraged in that direction. Folklore provides an opening to a difficult conversation. Rather than beginning with a discussion-stopper such as "Let's talk about gang rape," the legend of the frat boy's sister, while a very uncomfortable story to tell or hear, will create a better starting point.

Academics often complain about the speed with which textbooks become out of date. We know that in some ways this book is also becoming dated; as we are recording the legends and jokes used in this book, new ones are being generated and old ones are being modified. However, it doesn't matter, because the point is to make people aware of the range of folklore and how it can be used to enhance education. One of the great benefits of using contemporary folklore in education is that you don't need to rely on a textbook to provide the materials, so that the material used in class is as current as what students heard just yesterday or read on the Internet that morning. Unlike textbooks, folklore does not become out of date, unless you are only using material that has been mummified in a book, while ignoring its offspring which are repopulating the world of conversation, storytelling, and joketelling.

Even without directly using folklore in the classroom or other learning environments, an educator can benefit from paying attention to folklore. The second chapter in this book explored some of the ways folklore may inform us about the real or potential flaws in the educational process. In working with current or future sexuality educators, it has been very useful to tell some of the diaphragm/spermicidal jelly legends to illustrate the importance of specific and concrete explanations of birth control methods. Although some of these problems may be identified by discussing different learning styles, stories such as these provide a meaningful focal point. Next time you laugh at the equivalent of a "contraceptive jelly on toast" legend, it is worth examining the message behind it. Paying attention to folklore, especially beliefs, can also identify misunderstandings and incorrect beliefs. Often if these are examined, they provide a view into an even deeper level of misunderstanding—perhaps a fundamental misunderstanding—of human anatomy or physiology. Many of these beliefs would not normally surface in a classroom unless they are specifically solicited.

Specific Classroom and Clinical Approaches

Beliefs

One of the easiest ways to begin using folklore in sexuality education is by using beliefs. For any topic—menstruation, male and female changes at puberty, birth control, pregnancy, STDs, HIV/AIDS—students can be assigned to collect beliefs from family, peers, people in their community. Students should be carefully instructed to ask such questions as "What have you heard about . . . (what can prevent pregnancy, etc.)?" or "When you were a teenager, what did you hear about . . . ?" or "Before you moved to the United States, what did you hear about . . . ?" rather than "What do (or did) you believe about . . . ?" The former approach allows the recounting of beliefs without the informants' admitting their own beliefs or possibly revealing ignorance. Many informants make it clear that *they* don't accept certain beliefs but they know lots of people who do. Another important error to steer students away from is assum-

ing they know what the informant might believe ("Did you used to believe that you couldn't get pregnant if . . . ?") One of us (not the folklorist) made this classic tactical error in asking an older relative about
childbirth-related issues. The question "Did you ever use anything to
protect a newborn baby against the evil eye?" received a very strong and
discussion-stopping reply: "Only ignorant peasants believed that!" A
much better opening would have been, "Did you ever hear about anything some people used to do to protect a baby against the evil eye?"

To use these in class, students can hand in lists of the beliefs, which
the teacher can organize and categorize to avoid duplication, or students
can work in small groups and organize their own collections of beliefs.
The small groups could then research each belief, explaining why it is
or is not true, why people might believe it, and why it may be helpful
or harmful (whether or not it is true). To illustrate the latter, the belief
that a woman should urinate after intercourse to prevent pregnancy is
not true, but urinating after intercourse may be helpful in preventing
bladder infections. This exercise can work with a range of students, from
fifth and sixth graders studying puberty to college-level students studying HIV transmission. Some students may also wish to examine why
that belief might exist in a certain culture because of other cultural
beliefs or values. For example, a belief that monogamy prevents HIV
transmission helps reinforce the value placed on monogamy in that
culture, while leaving unexplored the complex definitions individuals
may have of monogamy and the fact that monogamy is not necessarily
protective. Another possibility for the small group activity can be to
develop ideas for health education that would help counter some of
the prevalent incorrect or dangerous beliefs. These ideas could be for
incorporation in the students' own classrooms, for a schoolwide health
education program, or for an even more extensive community program.

Another approach is to encourage students to write down beliefs to
contribute to an anonymous question box. Students often submit beliefs
to question boxes ("I've heard that . . . Is it true?") without encouragement, but making a special point of emphasizing beliefs may elicit some

additional contributions. The teacher can use these by having students do the research as suggested above or by providing the answers themselves. Questions and beliefs can be stored up until the appropriate moment arises in the curriculum.

It is also important for clinicians in health care settings to learn about beliefs of their clients. This can be approached in different ways. A health care provider can ask such questions as, "Why do you think you got sick?" which may be helpful in understanding a range of personal or cultural beliefs that could play an important role in how a client responds to recommendations for treatment or prevention. Although a health care practitioner may think he or she knows something about that particular culture, the assumption can't be made that every individual holds the same cultural beliefs. Sometimes presenters on multicultural health care and health education provide lists of different beliefs allegedly held by various groups. This approach is very limiting, since multicultural health education doesn't depend on learning lists, which can reinforce stereotypes of a group, while creating an unhelpful set of assumptions. Lists do not take into account diversity within a group or the flexibility of individuals. For example, one health text states that Jewish people do not mix meat and dairy products and won't eat pork or shellfish. This statement applies to Jews who keep strictly kosher and those who don't necessarily keep strictly kosher but are uncomfortable violating certain rules of kashrut, which leaves out a very large percentage of Jews. It would be better to ask individuals if there is anything they won't eat rather than assuming you know. In many different settings, learning the beliefs of the learners or clients is a key to providing a useful educational experience or the appropriate health care.

Without being an anthropologist, it is still possible for a health educator or clinician doing health education, one-on-one or in a group, to draw on individuals' cultural understandings of health issues, disease, and disease transmission. Writing about the Diversity in Medicine curriculum, a project conceived by David Hufford, a folklorist who teaches in a medical school, O'Connor (1997) explains:

Crucial to the curriculum content is the message that simplistic conceptions of diversity misrepresent actual human experience and reinforce stereotypes. Curriculum materials incorporate recognition that individuals belong to multiple identity groups (e.g., culture, gender, age, familial, professional, affinal), giving each person ("patient") a complex matrix of influences. Within groups, the experiences and needs of each individual, and the ways in which he or she selects from and interprets the available cultural repertoire, are unique. Cultural elements interact with individual lives and experiences, and diversity is often as great within groups as between and among them. The curriculum demonstrates to medical students that there is no such person as "the" native American patient or "the" female patient, and shows how cultural and other influences (as well as disease processes) play out in the lives and experiences of unique individuals. (P. 68)

Her article explains how folklore is used in this medical curriculum, emphasizing that "folklorists in medical schools are engaged in the business not of training physicians to be folklorists, but of contributing to training them to be better physicians" (O'Connor, 1997, p. 69).

In her book *The Spirit Catches You and You Fall Down*, Anne Fadiman (1997) recounts a true story of cultural conflicts and lack of communication in the interactions of a Hmong family with the health care system in California, which resulted in tragic consequences for a young girl with severe epilepsy. She suggests that Kleinman's questions (Kleinman, Eisenberg, and Good, 1978), used to elicit a patient's explanation of a disease process, might have helped avert many of the problems in the girl's (mis)treatment. After eliciting the patient's explanatory model, the clinician can work to negotiate with the patient about treatment. Some of the suggested questions are:

1. What do you think has caused the problem?
2. Why do you think it started when it did?

3. What do you think your sickness does? How does it work? (Kleinman, Eisenberg, and Good, 1978, p. 256)

Because these questions seem appropriate for groups whose culture may be seen to differ obviously from the majority of U.S. culture, it may be forgotten that we all belong to folk groups and have sets of beliefs. These questions can easily be used to elicit the beliefs about disease transmission or prevention from any client who has come in for treatment of an STD. Or variations could be used with a client who has come in for a pregnancy test and had not planned to become pregnant. The follow-up questions can elicit more specific details. For example, the dialogue might go like this:

Q. Were you doing anything to prevent pregnancy?
A. I was using a diaphragm.

Q. How do you think this approach works?
A. It prevents the sperm from getting to the egg by blocking the cervix.

Q. Why do you think it might not have worked this time?
A. I didn't use it for a few days.

Q. Why didn't you use it?
A. It was a safe time; I didn't need to.

Q. What do you believe is a safe time?
A. Any time after midway through my cycle.

This could then be a springboard for a discussion about cycles and safe times, which would be more useful than a lecture either on the importance of using contraception carefully or on the correct use of a diaphragm.

A story of cultural misunderstanding in the health care system, similar in some ways to that told by Fadiman, is related by David Hufford (1997), with an emphasis on what doctors need to learn:

No amount of cultural description will ever tell doctors all they need to know about patients within any community, although it provides very helpful background. Only learning to listen carefully to each patient while appreciating the multiple cultural frameworks involved, those of medicine and those of the patient's background, will allow each patient to receive the care they need. This kind of listening is one of the skills that ethnographers can teach. (P. 121)

And this is the kind of listening that occurs when a health care provider or health educator is aware of the potential role of folklore.

Legends

Legends also provide a very helpful context for approaching sexuality issues. A teacher can begin by explaining what legends are and assigning students to collect legends on specific topics to bring in for discussion. Another and often more successful starting point is to ask if anyone knows any stories about a certain topic and then later use examples to explain what legends are. Many people, considering themselves too sophisticated and educated, resist the idea that they and their friends share legends but will admit to having heard gross, weird, or bizarre stories. The emphasis in class, rather than being on whether or not something is a legend, should be on what can be learned from discussing it. One approach is the same as with the beliefs: No matter how improbable, could this have happened? Why or why not? From there the discussion can move to the question of what the legend can tell us about how a group of people are viewed (such as gay men as predators or fraternity men as rapists) and what is problematic about this kind of stereotyping. Legends also create an opportunity to discuss what people are afraid of or anxious about. As with beliefs, no one needs to say whether or not *they* believe them but why *other people* may.

Certainly, being aware of legends is important for anyone trying to provide public health education. A newspaper columnist (Marchione, 1999) recently wrote about problems with health-related stories on the Internet:

> This month, it's Febreze killing pets and aspartame causing Alzheimer's disease and multiple sclerosis. Last month it was HIV-tainted needles in movie theaters. Before that it was travelers being drugged and robbed of organs for black market transplantation.
>
> All are health-related hoaxes, myths, pranks, rumors and urban legends perpetuated through the Internet. They share these features: a medical claim that is not based on fact; a suggestion that the information came from an authoritative source such as police or health officials; and an intent or effect of causing panic and anxiety or damage to a product or institution's reputation. (P. G1)

Marchione's column is useful in pointing out that these are all undocumented, but she may not recognize that however and for whatever reasons a rumor/legend started, folklore is very powerful. Her column concludes: "People who spread false rumors on the Internet are no different than people who did it the old-fashioned way—by word of mouth. The tactic is unfair, and the results are damaging, no matter how they're achieved."

Most of the people who "spread" these are doing it in good faith. Often an e-mail is forwarded because someone genuinely believes it is true and wants to pass on the warning, often commenting that they think "it is for real." Public health educators need to keep responding to new legends/rumors as they arise, but it also is important to lay the groundwork so that as people hear or read these, they will have a context in which to understand them. If as part of health education, students learn about folklore, how it is transmitted and the functions it may serve, they are more likely to identify folklore when they see it. Even though, as we have pointed out, folklore is not necessarily false, awareness of folklore may help students become more skeptical readers of health information obtained from the Internet. While the column just cited may have helped educate a number of readers, an examination of these stories as folklore, rather than as individual acts by "people who spread false rumors," might have given readers additional tools for analyzing new material as they encounter it. Diane Goldstein, a folklorist who has extensively studied and written about the folklore of AIDS, presents some of the reasons for a collaboration between health educators and folklorists:

> Health educators, interestingly enough, seem to understand about genres even though they don't know what to call them or how they work. What they do know is that the form of messages determines their effectiveness. The folklorist has the ability contained in our knowledge of genres to show health educators how and why certain issues can only be appropriately articulated through certain expressive forms. AIDS education provides a clear example of genre choice as central to the ability to convey health information because issues of sexuality, intimacy and mortality are so clearly channeled into indirect discussion through narrative, joke, or graffiti. The folklorist has the ability to demonstrate the characteristics of genres and therefore to point to how and why communicative choices are made. Such choices affect not only how the lay population articulates health information, attitudes, and needs, but also spells out for health educators the forms that must be used for appropriate educational responses. (Goldstein, 1993, p. 20)

Jokes

Jokes are usually not viewed as a part of ongoing classroom activity, but rather as an interruption, sometimes welcome, or a diversion. Reactions may include laughter, lack of understanding, groans, comments about how gross or sick it was. It is rare for jokes to be incorporated into the classroom discussion. Of course nothing may ruin a joke faster than trying to explain why it's *funny;* discussing why a joke is *popular* is a better activity. It can create an opportunity to examine stereotypes, to provide correct information, to discuss why certain jokes may be painful and how they may undermine a group's fight for equality or social justice. For example, there have been many jokes about women enjoying rape and there are many about battered women now. While a teacher may not want to solicit such jokes, any of them that surface may provide a teachable moment. Other teachers, particularly in later high school or older, may want to have students bring in jokes to analyze.

Other Uses of Folklore in Education

Educators are finding a number of ways to use folklore in education. For example, one group, CARTS (Cultural Arts Resources for Teachers, www.carts.org) provides lists of books and other resources in such areas as Folklife and Arts Education, Urban Life and Culture, Children's Folklore. The resources cited provide guides to using folklore in the classroom. One very useful resource, *Folklore in the Classroom* (Belanus, 1985), presents short discussions, suggested classroom activities, and bibliographies for a number of subject areas. Other helpful resources include Bartis and Bowman (1994), Simons (1990), and *Folklife in Education* (1991). Classroom assignments for students may involve collecting folklore from their cultural group. These often focus on traditional folkways, material culture, or food culture, with discussions of how a group celebrates particular holidays, with demonstrations of dances, clothing, or food preparation. Other work may focus on oral histories with members of an individual's community, both to help the students understand their own culture and to help preserve some of the traditional information. Many teachers may see these activities as limited to certain areas, such as social studies or history, but a teacher who realizes that folklore deals with every aspect of life can, with creativity, integrate it into almost all of the curriculum.

Conclusion

We hope one outcome of this book is that educators begin to see the possibilities of using folklore in some new areas. While this book has focused on sexuality issues, all of health provides a rich area for folklore exploration, including topics such as alcohol, tobacco and other drugs, infectious diseases, nutrition, exercise. Beliefs, legends, jokes, anecdotes, and personal experience narratives all could play a role in different parts of the health curriculum, and a creative teacher may find that there is no part of the curriculum in which folklore is irrelevant. People of all ages and backgrounds seem to become enthusiastic about folklore, once they understand what it is. Discussions of our work on this book with friends, relatives, and colleagues in a wide range of fields have often elicited additional folklore and related literary material, quite often with e-mail follow-ups that begin with "I think this is one of those legends. . . ." Those discussions have created greater awareness of folklore and the role it plays in everyone's day-to-day life. We hope the book will do the same and help us all see ourselves as participants in folk traditions.

REFERENCES

AAUW. (1993). *Hostile hallways: The AAUW survey on sexual harassment in America's schools.* AAUW.

Advocate. (1997). Hate in homeroom, December 23, 14.

Alesia, T. (1999). Undercover cops trolling the Web. *Wisconsin State Journal,* December 19, 1A, 10A.

Anderson, K. (1997). The age of unreason: Welcome to the factual free-for-all. *The New Yorker,* February 3, 40–43.

Associated Press. (1997). Will Smith sees lots of conspiracies. *Wisconsin State Journal,* July 6, 7A.

————. (1998). I've gotten my revenge: HIV-positive woman vents anger with sex. *Athens Banner-Herald,* July 31.

Banks, J. A. (1997). *Educating citizens in a multicultural society.* New York: Teachers College Press.

Banks, R. (1997). Review of *Our guys: The Glen Ridge rape and the secret life of the perfect suburb. New York Times Book Review,* August 3, 7–8.

Bartis, P., and Bowman, P. (Ed.). (1994). *A teacher's guide to folklife resources for K-12 classrooms.* Publications of the American Folklife Center, no. 19. Washington, D.C.: Library of Congress.

Belanus, B. J. (1985). *Folklore in the classroom.* Indianapolis: Indiana Historical Bureau.

Bloor, M., Thomas, M., et al. (1998). *Differences in sexual risk behaviour between young men and women traveling abroad from the UK. Lancet, 352* (Issue 9141), 1664–68.

Bolton, R. (1992). AIDS and promiscuity: Muddles in the models. In R. Bolton and M. Singer (Eds.), *Rethinking AIDS prevention.* New York: Gordon & Breach, 7–85.

Boston Women's Health Book Collective. (1998). *Our bodies, ourselves for the new century.* New York: Simon & Schuster (Touchstone Books).

Boswell, A. A., and Spade, J. Z. (1996). Fraternities and collegiate rape culture: Why are some fraternities more dangerous places for women? *Gender & Society, 10*(2), 133–47.

Brunvand, J. H. (1981). *The vanishing hitchhiker*. New York: W. W. Norton.

————. (1984). *The choking doberman*. New York: W. W. Norton.

Cassidy, F. G. (1985). *Dictionary of American regional English*. Volume I, *Introduction and A–C*. Cambridge, Mass.: Belknap Press of Harvard University Press.

Chicago Tribune. (1995). Lawmaker's remark on rape angers many. April 21, 4.

Chronicle of Higher Education. (1997). Fraternity indicted after alleged hazing. January 10, A8.

Clines, F. X. (1999). Barracks life of gay harassment is detailed at trial. *New York Times*, December 12, 21.

Cohen, M. R. (1987). Medication error reports. *Hospital Pharmacy, 22*(9), 955–57.

Collective Members of Massachusetts Asian AIDS Prevention Project (R. Sripada-Vaz and S. Lourcock [Eds.]). (1998). Expanding health options for Asian and Pacific Island women. *Sojourner,* March, *23*(7), 32.

Delaney, J., Lupton, M. J., and Toth, E. (1988). *The curse: A cultural history of menstruation*. Urbana and Chicago: University of Illinois Press.

Denney, N. W., and Quadagno, D. (1988). *Human sexuality*. St. Louis: Times Mirror/Mosby.

DiClemente, R. J., Zorn, J., and Temoshok, L. (1986). Adolescents and AIDS: A survey of knowledge, attitudes and beliefs about AIDS in San Francisco. *American Journal of Public Health, 76*(12), 1443–45.

Dresser, N. (1994). The case of the missing gerbil. *Western Folklore, 53,* 229–42.

Dusenbury, L., Botvin, G. J., Baker, E., and Laurence, J. (1991). AIDS risk knowledge, attitudes and behavior intentions among multi-ethnic adolescents. *AIDS Education and Prevention, 3*(4), 367–75.

Educator's Guide to Controlling Sexual Harassment. (1997). School district reaches settlement with former student for over $900,000. *4*(5), 1–2.

Ellis, B. (1997). Just in! Cybersex surpriser surprised. *FoafTale News, 42* (May), 13.

Fadiman, A. (1997). *The spirit catches you and you fall down: A Hmong child, her American doctors, and the collision of two cultures*. New York: Noonday Press, Farrar, Straus, and Giroux.

Fine, G. A. (1992). *Manufacturing tales: Sex and money in contemporary legends*. Knoxville: University of Tennessee Press.

Fleming, R. (1994). Just in! 19 July 1994. *FoafTale News, 35* (October), 10.

Folklife in Education. (1991). Special issue of *Southern Folklore, 48*(1).

Frank, B. (1999). Shepard murder clamors for anti-hate education. *Harvard Gay and Lesbian Review,* Winter, 4–5.

Gamble, V. N. (1997). Under the shadow of Tuskegee: African Americans and health care. *American Journal of Public Health, 87*(11), 1773–78.

Gibbs, H., and Ross, A. D. (1996). *The medicine of ER or, how we almost die.* New York: Basic Books.

Goldstein, D. (1992). Welcome to the mainland, welcome to the world of AIDS: Cultural viability, localization, and contemporary legend. *Contemporary Legend, 2,* 23–40.

———. (1993). Not just a "glorified anthropologist": Medical problem solving through verbal and material art. *Folklore in Use: Applications in the Real World, 1,* 15–24.

Goldstuck, A. (1994). Electronic communication on folklore discussion list. April 1, 1994.

Goodwin, J. P. (1989a). *More man than you'll ever be: Gay folklore and acculturation in middle America.* Bloomington: Indiana University Press.

———. (1989b). Unprintable reactions to all the news that's fit to print. *Southern Folklore, 46,* 15–39.

Goska, D. (1997). "Waking up less than whole": The female perpetrator in male-victim kidney-theft legends. *Southern Folklore, 54*(3), 196–210.

Greenberg, J. S. (1985). Iatrogenic health education disease. *Health Education, 16,* 4–6.

Grider, S. (1984). The razor blades in the apples syndrome. In P. Smith (Ed.), *Perspectives on contemporary legend: Proceedings of the conference on contemporary legends, Sheffield, July 1982.* Sheffield: University of Sheffield, 128–40.

Hall, L. A. (1991). *Hidden anxieties: Male sexuality, 1900–1950.* Cambridge: Polity Press.

Hathaway, R. (1997). Just in! Cybersex surpriser surprised. *FoafTale News, 42* (May), 12–13.

Healey, P., and Glanvill, R. (1996). *Now! That's what I call urban myths.* London: Virgin Books.

Henken, E. R., and Whatley, M. H. (1995). Folklore, legends, and sexuality education. *Journal of Sex Education and Therapy, 21*(1), 46–61.

Hiscock, P. (1998). Like a bowlful of jelly. *FoafTale News, 43* (February), 16–17.

Hufford, D. (1997). Gender, culture and experience: A painful case. *Southern Folklore, 54*(2), 114–23.

Jensen, T. K., et al. (1998). Does moderate alcohol consumption affect fertility? Follow up study among couples planning first pregnancy. *British Medical Journal, 317* (August 22) 505–10.

Kelly, D. (1994). Menstruation and bears. Http://www.urbanlegends.com/animals/menstruation_and_bears.html.

Kirby, D. (1997). *No easy answers: Research on programs to prevent teen pregnancy.* Washington, D.C.: National Campaign to Prevent Teen Pregnancy.

Kisker, E. E. (1985). Teenagers talk about sex, pregnancy, and contraception. *Family Planning Perspectives, 17*(2), 83–90.

Kleinman, A., Eisenberg, L., and Good, B. (1978). Culture, illness, and care: Clinical lessons from anthropologic and cross-cultural research. *Annals of Internal Medicine, 88,* 251–58.

Kondora, L. (1997). *A textual analysis of the construction of the false memory syndrome: Representations in popular magazines, 1990–95.* Ph.D. dissertation, University of Wisconsin-Madison.

Kozol, W. (1995). Fracturing domesticity: Media, nationalism, and the question of feminist influence. *Signs: Journal of Women in Culture and Society, 20,* 646–67.

Landers, A. (1997). That's not what they meant by oral contraceptive. *Wisconsin State Journal,* October 5.

Langlois, J. (1991). "Hold the mayo": Purity and danger in an AIDS legend. *Contemporary Legend, 1,* 153–72.

Manzione, E. (1996). High school AIDS rumor debunked. *Athens Observer* (Athens, GA), June 13–19, 1, 12A.

Marchione, M. (1999). Medical pranks tangle up truth on the Web. *Milwaukee Journal Sentinel,* April 19, G1.

Martin, E. (1991). The egg and the sperm: How science has constructed a romance based on stereotypical male-female roles. *Signs: Journal of Women in Culture and Society, 16*(3), 485–501.

Miller, E. K. (1993). Politics and gender: Geraldine Ferraro in the editorial cartoons. In S. T. Hollis, L. Pershing, and M. J. Young (Eds.), *Feminist theory and the study of folklore.* Urbana and Chicago: University of Illinois Press.

National Coalition Against Sexual Assault. (1997). New color-releasing formulation of Rohypnol announced at national NCASA meeting. News release from NCASA, October 16, 1997.

O'Connor, B. B. (1991). Applied belief studies and AIDS. In D. Goldstein (Ed.), *Talking AIDS.* ISER Research and Policy Papers, no. 12. St. John's: Memorial University of Newfoundland, 86.

————. (1997). Applying folklore in medical education. *Southern Folklore, 54*(2), 67–77.

Ostrov, E., Offer, D., Howard, K. I., Kaufman, B., and Meyer, H. (1985). Adolescent sexual behavior. *Medical Aspects of Human Sexuality, 19*(5), 28–31, 34–36.

Padian, N. S., Shiboski, S. C., and Jewell, N. P. (1991). Female-to-male transmission of human immunodeficiency virus. *Journal of the American Medical Association, 266*(12), 1664–67.

Pershing, L. (1996). His wife seized his prize and cut it to size: Folk and popular commentary on Lorena Bobbit. *NWSA Journal, 8*(3), 1–35.

Plunket, R. (1997). Review of *Gossip. New York Times Book Review,* June 1, 26.

Randolph, V. (1992). *Blow the candle out: "Unprintable" Ozark folksongs and folklore.* 2 volumes. G. Legman (Ed.). Fayetteville: University of Arkansas Press.

Response. (1999). Egyptian press update "The big lie." *20*(1), 9–10.

Rogers, L. L., Wilker, G. A., and Scott, S. S. (1991). Reactions of black bears to human menstrual odors. *Journal of Wildlife Management, 55*(4), 632–34.

Safe Schools Coalition. (1999). *They don't even know me: Understanding anti-gay harassment and violence in schools.* Seattle: Safe Schools Coalition. (Website: http://www.safeschools-wa.org).

Sanday, P. R. (1990). *Fraternity gang rape: Sex, brotherhood, and privilege on campus.* New York: New York University Press.

Sanders, S. A., and Reinisch, J. M. (1999). Would you say you "had sex" if . . . ? *JAMA, 282*(3), 275–77.

Schoepf, B. G. (1995). Culture, sex research, and AIDS prevention in Africa. In H. ten Brummelhuis and G. Herdt (Eds.), *Culture and sexual risk: Anthropological perspectives on AIDS.* Australia: Gordon and Breach, 29–51.

Scott, J. R. (1995). Do the tentacles go into the virginia? And other questions 4th, 5th, and 6th grade students ask, if given the opportunity, and how teachers might answer them. Master's thesis, Department of Curriculum and Instruction, University of Wisconsin-Madison.

Sears, J. T. (1997). Centering culture: Teaching for critical sexual literacy using the sexual diversity wheel. *Journal of Moral Education, 26*(3), 273–83.

Shelby, A. (1999). The "R" word: What's so funny (and not so funny) about redneck jokes. In D. B. Billings and K. Ledford (Eds.), *Confronting Appalachian stereotypes: Back talk from an American region.* Lexington: University of Kentucky Press, 153–60.

Shilts, R. (1987). *And the band played on: Politics, people, and the AIDS epidemic.* New York: St. Martin's Press.

Simons, E. R. (1990). *Student worlds, student words: Teaching writing through folklore*. Portsmouth, N.H.: Boynton/Cook-Heinemann.

Simpson, M. (1994). *Male impersonators: Men performing masculinity*. New York: Routledge.

Sloane, E. (1993). *The biology of women*. 3d ed. Albany: Delmar Publishers.

Sobo, E. J. (1995). *Choosing unsafe sex: AIDS-risk denial among disadvantaged women*. Philadelphia: University of Pennsylvania Press.

————. (1997). Menstrual taboos, witchcraft, babies, and social relations: Women's health traditions in rural Jamaica. In C. Lopez Springfield (Ed.), *Daughters of Caliban: Caribbean women in the twentieth century*. Bloomington: Indiana University Press, 143–70.

Stu. (1994). Just in! 9 June 1994. *FoafTale News, 35* (October), 10.

Taberner, P. V. (1985). *Aphrodisiacs: The science and the myth*. Philadelphia: University of Pennsylvania Press.

Thompson, S. (1995). *Going all the way: Teenage girls' tales of sex, romance, and pregnancy*. New York: Hill and Wang.

Travis, J. (1997). Why do women menstruate? *Science News, 151* (15), 230–31.

Turner, P. A. (1993). *I heard it through the grapevine: Rumor in African-American culture*. Berkeley: University of California Press.

Tweeten, S. S. M., and Rickman, L. S. (1998). Infectious complications of body piercing. *Clinical Infectious Diseases, 26* (March), 267–68.

Van Buren, A. (2000). Mountain Dew doesn't act as a contraceptive. *Cedar Rapids Gazette*. March 26.

Vorpagel, B. (1988). A rodent by any other name: Implications of a contemporary legend. *International Folklore Review, 6,* 53–7.

Will, G. F. (2000). AIDS crushes a continent. *Newsweek,* January 10, 64.

Wright, J. (1998). *Lesbian step families: An ethnography of love*. New York: Harrington Park Press.

Zelnik, M., and Kantner, J. F. (1979). Reasons for nonuse of contraception by sexually active women aged 15–19. *Family Planning Perspectives, 11*(5), 289–96.

INDEX

ABOUT THE AUTHORS

Mariamne H. Whatley is a Professor of Women's Studies and Curriculum & Instruction at the University of Wisconsin-Madison. She has an A.B. in English from Radcliffe College–Harvard University and her Ph.D. in Biological Sciences from Northwestern University. Her research and teaching interests include women's health issues and sexuality education.

Elissa R. Henken earned her A.B. in Folklore and Mythology at Radcliffe College–Harvard University, her M.A. in Welsh Language and Literature at the University College of Wales, Aberystwyth, and her Ph.D. at the Folklore Institute at Indiana University. She now teaches Folklore and Celtic literature as a Professor in the Department of English at the University of Georgia.